D. W.
Winnicott

Key Figures in Counselling and Psychotherapy

Series editor: Windy Dryden

The *Key Figures in Counselling and Psychotherapy* series of books provides a concise, accessible introduction to the lives, contributions and influence of the leading innovators whose theoretical and practical work has had a profound impact on counselling and psychotherapy. The series includes comprehensive overviews of:

Sigmund Freud
by Michael Jacobs

Eric Berne
by Ian Stewart

Carl Rogers
by Brian Thorne

Melanie Klein
by Julia Segal

Fritz Perls
by Petrūska Clarkson and Jennifer Mackewn

Aaron T. Beck
by Marjorie E. Weishaar

Albert Ellis
by Joseph Yankura and Windy Dryden

Joseph Wolpe
by Roger Poppen

George Kelly
by Fay Fransella

D. W. Winnicott
by Michael Jacobs

D.W.
Winnicott

Michael Jacobs

SAGE Publications
London ● Thousand Oaks ● New Delhi

First published 1995
Reprinted 1998, 2001, 2003, 2006

SAGE Publications Ltd.
1 Oliver's Yard, 55 City Road
London EC1Y 1SP

SAGE Publications Inc
2455 Teller Road
Thousand Oaks, California 91320

SAGE Publications India Pvt Ltd.
B-42 Panchsheel Enclave
Post Box 4109
New Delhi 110 017

British Library Cataloguing in Publication Data

A catalogue record for this book is available
from the British Library

ISBN 10: 0-8039-8595-9   ISBN 13: 978-0-8039-8595-7
ISBN 10: 0-8039-8596-7 (pbk)   ISBN 13: 978-0-8039-8596-4 (pbk)

Library of Congress catalog card number 95–71212

Typeset by Mayhew Typesetting, Rhayader, Powys
Printed and bound in Great Britain by
Athenaeum Press Ltd., Gateshead, Tyne & Wear.

Contents

Preface

When the series editor offered me the opportunity to write about
D. W. Winnicott, he gave me the chance to learn as much as I had
done in writing about Freud, for the first volume in this series. As
with that book, he provided me with the incentive to read more
widely and more thoroughly in the considerable literature by and
on Winnicott, whom I had up to that point quoted with obvious
relish whenever I wished to find legitimacy for a less than orthodox
view on psychoanalytic theory or practice. As I suggest in the
closing paragraphs (which at this point are to the reader yet a long
way off), I think I may not have been alone in using his name in
this way. When teaching a course at the time of writing the
concluding chapter, I commented to the group upon the informality
with which Winnicott greeted Guntrip at the start of Guntrip's
therapy sessions. The response from one course member illustrated
a second way in which his name is used. She said, 'Ah, but
Winnicott was Winnicott.' In other words, there are unorthodox
ways in psychoanalysis, and that shows how progressive it is, but
they are not for the likes of us. At first I was tempted to respond in
turn that we are all Winnicotts, although I suspect that this would
not have been in the spirit of the man. 'We are all ourselves, and we
might actually need to become ourselves' would possibly have been
a more appropriate reply, had I at the time thought quickly enough.

In fact, as I discovered when I read through the sources on his
life, Winnicott was not as unorthodox as I had imagined. The
picture is a complex one, just as the politics of psychoanalysis is
complicated, and he needs to be understood against that background. I have discovered the appropriateness of questioning both
him and his ideas – more so than I had at first contemplated. I have
also found a welcome for a critical stance from many of those
whom I have consulted. Those who have studied Winnicott in
depth do not idolize him in the way many of us who have casually
quoted him sometimes appear to do. That has been both a relief for
the writer and an incentive to do him justice.

There were fewer resources than I had at my disposal for my

earlier text on Freud. The books by Davis and Wallbridge (1981) and by Phillips (1988) provided clear pathways into the many ideas that Winnicott had generated. Here and there were other texts, which threw light upon his life, and which examined his theory and practice from different perspectives. I had at my disposal more of his papers in published form than I suspect Phillips had, even though Davis and Wallbridge would have had access to the same material in original documents and papers. I have also had the opportunity of meeting people who knew Winnicott personally, or who have devoted more time to the study of his work than I could ever have done in the relatively short time involved in writing this book. Such interviews gave me a taste of what it must be like to write a biography, especially the delight I experienced in talking with those who have valued Winnicott in person, or who so obviously enjoy their contact with his thinking. While hoping that one day there may be a more comprehensive and critical biography than has yet appeared, I had in my own less extensive researches a sense of what fascinating material and memories await such fashioning.

The limited nature of my knowledge before I embarked upon my own writing here has meant that I have appreciated, even more than I did in the preparation of my other books, generous sharing of information and ideas, advice on sources and refinement of my sometimes inadequate comprehension. This has come from a number of people, some of whom I have met for the first time. I am grateful that this project gave me the opportunity to do so. My particular thanks go to Professor John Davis, who rightly cherishes not only both the Winnicotts but also his late wife's superb contribution to the editing and explanations of Winnicott's papers; to Professor Windy Dryden who gave me the opening for this subject, and whose editing of the text has been gentler than I have experienced before, leading me to hope that my grammar and sentence construction improve with age; to Nina Farhi and Louise Exeter – respectively director and general secretary of the Squiggle Foundation – for all manner of help from start to finish; to Dr Isobel Hunter-Brown and to the librarian of the Institute of Psycho-Analysis for searching out and supplying papers and chapters critical of and influenced by Winnicott; to Dr Peter Lomas for reading the text from another perspective and ensuring that I recognized both strengths and shortcomings in Winnicott's writing; to Dr Lynne Murray and Sheelah Seeley – director and researcher respectively at the Winnicott Research Unit in Cambridge – for explaining so fully their studies of as well as their work with mothers and babies, and for generously allowing me to draw upon their published and unpublished papers; and at the end of the alphabet, but in fact always there from A through to Z, my wife Moira Walker, whose judgement I always value, and whose love provides the best facilitating environment of all.

Michael Jacobs
Leicester

1
The Life of D. W. Winnicott

There are in public life and letters certain figures who catch the imagination and evoke admiration, sometimes only on the basis of a small number of known facts about them, and a few well-chosen phrases uttered by them. Most of us in fact know little about such figures, although we imagine we know them well, because their names are frequently dropped into conversations. We quote them, as evidence of basic truths we hold important, although in truth we probably only have a few phrases of theirs in our minds, what modern jargon might call 'sound-bites'. We have probably never read their books.

In the allied fields of counselling and psychotherapy one such figure is D. W. Winnicott. Although those who were close to him call him Donald, 'D. W.' or 'D. W. W.' for the rest of us he is 'Winnicott' – just as in the completely different medium of television, one that he himself appeared to have enjoyed, we think of 'Morse' or 'Lovejoy'. They have no first names, and we probably do not even think of his first names – Donald Woods. Although those close to him appear to revere his memory with enormous love and with a fund of stories about him that at times make him appear a saint, to most of us his life is sketchy, even if we quote him and speak about his work with a similar degree of praise. Some of the terms he coined trip off our tongues in discussions, in lectures and in supervision – notably 'the good-enough mother', 'the transitional object', 'true and false self', 'the facilitating environment' and perhaps 'there is no such thing as a baby'. We have in fact for the most part, especially if we come from outside psychoanalytic circles, slender acquaintance with his written work, except perhaps the best-selling *The Child, the Family and the Outside World* (1964), or one or two of his occasional papers, such as 'Hate in the Counter-Transference' (1975).

This is of course not an unusual phenomenon in the world of counselling and therapy. Each school has its idols: Freud, Klein and Rogers became such and largely remain such, on a scale which probably exceeds Winnicott. They are similarly introduced to the reader in their own volumes in this series. All of these figures – and more – have been focuses for a minor industry of training and writing. There are signs that Winnicott too has become another of those whose ideas and techniques are about to spawn another shelf of books, although far less obviously a school of training and practice. The Winnicott Trust has encouraged the publication of all his papers left at the time of his death, a collection which is all but complete. They have however resisted so far the idea of a 'Collected Works', uncertain if that is what Winnicott would have wished. Alongside the increasing volume of literature on the history and thinking of psychoanalysis and psychoanalysts, attention is constantly turned to Winnicott's work. This present volume is one of many that are being written about his ideas and his practice, although unlike this one, many of them address those already familiar with current psychoanalytic thinking.

As yet there has been no definitive biography. Winnicott's American disciple Robert Rodman was turned down by the then members of the Winnicott Trust when he sought permission some years ago for access to the papers for such a work. For the most part, references to Winnicott's life appear disappointingly repetitious in the various books that refer to his own development. They turn out in the end to be based for the most part on the reminiscences of his second wife, Clare Winnicott. These appear in her 'D. W. W.: A Reflection' in one of the earliest volumes of papers assessing Winnicott's ideas (Grolnick et al., 1978); and in an interview recorded in 1983 and reprinted in Rudnytsky (1991). She refers also, as do most 'lives', to the few pages of an autobiography that Winnicott had started to write shortly before his death. There are, of course, also personal references in his papers, where Winnicott is refreshingly open about himself and his own responses to situations. There is little attempt to present a faceless 'objective' picture, especially since he writes so often from and of his clinical practice. Some of his extensive correspondence has been published (Rodman, 1987), and this helps to build up a more comprehensive picture of a man who wrote generously to those who communicated with him (although quite critically at times to those to whom he wished to communicate his passionate views). There are a few tantalizingly brief references to his life in some of the writing of his close colleague Masud Khan (such as the preface, curiously inaccurate in places, to Clancier and Kalmanovitch, 1987) and disguised allusions to him (as the mysterious Mr X) in Marion Milner's extensive case study *In the Hands of the Living God* (1969). Adam Phillips's useful summary of Winnicott's life and ideas (1988) is rather fuller, although it still largely draws on the same relatively narrow sources.

An introduction to Winnicott's ideas and practice has therefore considerable material to draw upon in his papers and books, now virtually all published. But without the help of a full biography the man himself remains (to those who did not know him personally and well) less than complete. It seems as if the reader and this author must await a more searching examination of Winnicott's life, although I share here as much as in the context of an introductory work I can usefully glean. What I have found myself asking is why Winnicott and his particular expression of psychoanalytic thought exerts such a fascination for many counsellors and therapists, including those who would not necessarily wish to associate themselves with the British Institute of Psycho-Analysis? The answer to that searching question must lie partly in the sort of person he was, although, as I shortly show, any full-scale biographer needs to get behind the near-ideal picture painted of him.

Early Life

That Winnicott should be such a 'favourite' thinker for counsellors and therapists makes immediate sense when we learn that he was also a highly favoured child. Other authors also attach significance to the location of his upbringing. Donald Woods Winnicott was born on 7 April 1896, in Plymouth, which they remind us was the final setting-out place of the Pilgrim Fathers on their journey to America. Plymouth may therefore symbolize a tradition of dissent (Phillips, 1988: 23), although Winnicott's own dissenting nature may also come partly from being brought up in a favoured position – it can lead to a confidence which makes less likely the need to conform to gain acceptance. Certainly Winnicott's later refusal to be tied to one way of thinking makes him, for a variety of reasons, an attractive figure to counsellors and therapists who similarly favour autonomy or self-actualization, or whatever term they employ in their basic philosophy.

He was the youngest of three children, and the only son. His father is described variously as a corsetry merchant, according to Phillips (1988), or as a wholesaler in hardware who supplied the Navy, by Clare Winnicott (Rudnytsky, 1991: 184). In due course his father became Lord Mayor of Plymouth, a magistrate, and was subsequently knighted. Sir Frederick is described as having 'an old-fashioned quiet dignity and poise about him, and a deep sense of fun. Those who knew him speak of him as a person of high intelligence and sound judgement' despite, as Winnicott described him, his having had learning difficulties (Grolnick et al., 1978: 21, 23). Although he was (as I describe later) clearly remembered by

Winnicott with great affection as being present after church on Sundays, his father was not so obviously present at other times. Winnicott, looking back, felt that he did not see enough of his father, saying, 'I was left too much to all my mothers. Thank goodness I was sent away at thirteen!' (Rudnytsky, 1991: 185). Perhaps his father's absence through work and in civic duties – not of course untypical of the time or indeed of fathers' relative absence generally – creeps into Winnicott's writing about men and into his theoretical position on the significance of father. This I outline in Chapter 2 and examine more critically in Chapter 4.

The reference above to 'all my mothers' probably stems from the young Donald being brought up in a household of women: his mother, two sisters six and seven years older than him, a nanny, sometimes a governess and an aunt who lived with the family for much of the time. Across the road was another Winnicott household – his uncle's – with three boys among the five cousins there. He was devoted to his nanny, and Clare Winnicott remembered them seeking her out in London in 1950, to 'ensure she was all right and living comfortably' (Grolnick et al., 1978: 21). Letters home to his mother later in adolescence also reveal similar affection.

Winnicott's upbringing was in a Methodist home. Both his parents were leading members of the local Methodist church, his father being both treasurer and in the choir. This non-conformist background is important, particularly for the type of non-conformity it represented, which was of an independent spirit, and yet not narrow-minded and repressive in the way some non-conformist religion can be. It was his father who was the life-long Methodist. Winnicott's mother had been an Anglican before her marriage, as he himself was to become while he was at medical school. (Winnicott's first wife was also an Anglican and Clare Winnicott remembers that as the occasion for Winnicott being confirmed, at the age of 26 or 27, although she says that he did not go to church for very long.)

The Methodist church was a few minutes walk away. Clare Winnicott tells the story of how Donald used to walk home from church with his father: this was experienced as a privilege for the youngest in the family. Donald started his father talking about religion, asking him a question about it. His father apparently replied, 'Listen, my boy. You read the Bible – what you find there. And you decide for yourself what you want, you know. It's free. You don't have to believe what I think. Make up your own mind about it. Just read the Bible' (Rudnytsky, 1991: 180–1). Later Winnicott was to describe how 'I am always glad that my religious upbringing was of a kind that allowed for *growing up out of*' (Winnicott, 1986:

143, my italics). This over-prepositioned phrase (but again one of those memorable snatches of Winnicott's prose) in fact triples the direction of the growth, and aptly describes Winnicott's attitude to the need to outgrow dogma in psychoanalysis as much as in religion. Although later Winnicott no longer described himself as a Christian, the idea of belief remained vital to him. Clare Winnicott recalled him saying, 'The point is, can they believe? I don't care what it's about. The capacity to believe is more important than what you believe' (Rudnytsky, 1991: 181).

As the youngest child and only boy, Donald received much attention from 'a lot of people who thought he was wonderful' (Rudnytsky, 1991: 180). It seems to have been also a good home to 'grow up out of'. Everyone had a great sense of humour. 'There weren't disasters in the Winnicott home . . . just funny episodes' (Rudnytsky, 1991: 181). Donald had no doubts he was loved, and this engendered a deep sense of security. As Clare Winnicott puts it: 'from this basic position Donald was then free to explore all the available spaces in the house and garden around him and to fill the spaces with bits of himself and so gradually make his world his own. This capacity *to be at home* served him well throughout his life' (Grolnick et al., 1978: 21). Later in life she recalled how when travelling abroad he would often be found in the kitchen of an inn. As a child, his mother apparently complained, he spent more time with the cook in the kitchen than in the rest of the house.

There is a sense of near-idealization in Clare Winnicott's descriptions of the different aspects of Winnicott's childhood, set in a family home which appears to have all the appearance of normality enriched with warm feelings and good relationships. One wonders how much his devoted widow paints a portrait which if mostly true is nonetheless selective and seductive, and whether she reads back into his early life all the positive feelings she was herself left with. One of my sources who knew both Donald and Clare Winnicott commented (in a personal communication) that she 'kept up an ideal picture of Donald and didn't give the low-down', although another source cites what may or may not be an apocryphal comment of Clare Winnicott's that Winnicott had 'delusions of benignity'. Even then his naughtiness (and it is no more than that) is told in a way which seems intended to charm. Is it the cynicism bred by psychoanalytic thinking that makes the reader ask where the more negative side is? Clare Winnicott was herself aware of this:

> Some who read this abbreviated account of D. W. W.'s early life and
> family relationships may be inclined to think it sounds too good to be

true. But the truth is that it *was* good, and try as I will I cannot present it in any other light. Essentially he was a deeply happy person whose capacity for enjoyment never failed to triumph over the setbacks and disappointments that came his way. Moreover there is a sense in which the quality of his early life and his appreciation of it did present him with a major problem, that of freeing himself from the family and establishing his own separate life and identity without sacrificing the early richness. It took him a long time to do this. (Grolnick et al., 1978: 25)

We might therefore sympathize with the nine-year-old Donald, who we are told looked in the mirror and said 'I'm too nice', and from that point determined to show another side of himself. He started becoming bottom of the class; and he pulled the wings off flies, although such behaviour is far from the deviancy and delinquency that he was later to work with and write about. 'He wanted to find this other dimension in himself' (Rudnytsky, 1991: 186); feeling too good and too much liked by everybody, he had to find the nastiness in himself. Clare tells also of an episode when Donald was three, when he smashed his sister's doll's face with a mallet, a doll that his father used to tease him with. Winnicott himself wrote of this incident that 'much of my life has been founded on the undoubted fact that I actually *did* this deed, not merely wished it and planned it' (Grolnick et al., 1978: 23). He was also relieved when his father melted the doll's waxen nose and repaired it so that it became a face again. It was an early demonstration of the power of the reparative act, that in itself helped him to accept that he had actually become violent both with the doll and, indirectly, with his father. Reparation is another of the themes Winnicott was to stress in his work. But repairing alone might miss another significant aspect of this wilfulness:

Toleration of one's destructive impulses results in a new thing: the capacity to enjoy ideas, even with destruction in them, and the bodily excitements that belong to them, or that they belong to. This development gives elbow-room for the experience of concern, which is the basis for everything constructive. (Winnicott, 1986: 87)

It was another moment of wilfulness that seemed to the young Winnicott to be the reason (although clearly in retrospect not the real reason) for him being sent away to boarding school. He was at that time at a preparatory school in Plymouth, and he recalls that one day he came home to midday dinner and said 'drat'. 'My father looked pained as only he could look, blamed my mother for not seeing to it that I had decent friends, and from that moment he prepared himself to send me away' (Grolnick et al., 1978: 23). So at thirteen, the usual age for public schoolboys, Donald Winnicott went to the Leys School in Cambridge – a non-conformist foundation. He may have missed home, but he quickly entered with enthusiasm into this new experience, and he appears to have 'loved' public school life. 'He had immense vitality and capacity to enter into things and enjoy himself. I've never known anyone who could enjoy himself more', said his widow Clare, again in glowing terms (Rudnytsky, 1991: 181). He wrote many letters home, all of which show his 'liveliness and interest' (Rudnytsky, 1991: 185), sending his love to everyone including the cat and the maids. The family had given him the security to become free enough to explore and to embrace new experiences. The idea of 'playing' started early, and not surprisingly therefore assumes great significance in Winnicott's writing and in his actual practice. He ran, cycled, swam, played rugger, joined the Scouts and sang in the choir.

Discovering Darwin and Freud

It was when he was at this school, as he described in a talk given in 1945 to sixth-formers (1957: 128–9), that Winnicott discovered Darwin's *Origin of Species*. He found the books in second-hand shops in Cambridge, and in time collected all Darwin's work. In a letter to his mother he says that he would like money for his birthday 'to buy some of those wonderful books I pass every day' (Rudnytsky, 1991: 182). Of the *Origin of Species* in particular he said, 'I could not leave off reading it.' Looking back he thought that 'the main thing was that it showed that living things could be examined scientifically with the corollary that gaps in knowledge and understanding need not scare me' (1957: 129). In this there are two further pointers to his later work. Firstly, the importance of the environment and of adaptation to it. But unlike Larmarckian theory that sees species as capable of adapting themselves to changes in the environment, Darwin's theory of natural selection means that it is not easy to survive in a hostile environment. If it is only by chance that mutants of a species may find themselves more suited for the changing environment, it is also true that the stability of the environment is essential for normal survival and growth. Babies cannot adapt: they need a facilitating environment. This was to provide a counter to the over-concentration upon internal experience that tended to dominate British psychoanalytic thought once Melanie Klein's theories held sway during the 1930s. At the same time Darwin's theory gave Winnicott a deep belief in the developmental process and in the drive towards health, including mental health.

The second pointer to Winnicott's later work to be found in his early interest in Darwin is finding that 'gaps in knowledge and understanding need not scare me' (1957: 129). The importance for him and his work of the gaps, or, in his more considered language, the spaces in between, becomes clearer in later chapters. So too does his willingness to accept not understanding. In a comment on one of the early consultations with 'the Piggle' (see Chapter 3) Winnicott wrote: 'Importance of my not *understanding* what she has not yet been able to give me clues for. Only she knew the answers, and when she could encompass the meaning of the fears she would make it possible for me to understand too' (1980: 48). Clare Winnicott felt that Darwin changed Winnicott's attitude to religion and indeed changed his whole life. The scientific way of working excited him, and made him feel that this was what he wanted to pursue. He remained of the view that psychoanalysis was a science, writing in 1946 to Ella Freeman Sharpe: 'I enjoy true psycho-analytic work more than the other kinds, and the reason is to some extent bound up with the fact that in psycho-analysis the art is less and the technique is based on scientific considerations more' (Rodman, 1987: 10). Yet his considerable and innovative contribution to the discipline seems rather less scientifically rigorous than others who have also claimed the same status for psychoanalysis. His use of observation may have been greater than that of many in the field, but some of his hypotheses (perhaps inevitably, given the difficulty of describing infant experience) involve leaps of faith. He was fully aware that there were objections to calling psychology a science because of the highly subjective element in observations, especially through the influence of the repressed unconscious. Nevertheless psychoanalysis is still 'an instrument of scientific research' (1957: 133). Chapter 5 considers some of the more scientifically rigorous psychological research that has been applied to some of Winnicott's hypotheses.

It is interesting to find a reference to unconscious communication, perhaps before he had even heard of Freud, in a letter written to a school friend, when Winnicott was only sixteen: 'Father and I have been trying consciously and perhaps unconsciously to find out what the ambition of the other is in regard to my future' (Grolnick et al., 1978: 25). His growing interest in science meant turning down the idea that he should go into his father's business, which he knew his father expected him to do – eventually to take it over from him. He was keen to please his father, but a friend persuaded him (as indeed his father might also have done) that he had to do what he wanted. The same letter refers to Winnicott's own wish: 'I have for ever so long wanted to be a doctor.' One of the factors in this may have been his breaking a collar bone on the sports field at school (Khan refers instead to a damaged hip, but this appears to be one of a number of confusions in Khan's memory: he also refers to Winnicott's father as 'George' rather than 'Frederick' (Clancier and Kalmanovitch, 1987: xvi)). Clare Winnicott recalled how he had often said with reference to that time: 'I could see that for the rest of my life I would have to depend on doctors if I damaged myself or became ill, and the only way out of this position was to become a doctor myself' (Grolnick et al., 1978: 25). We might wonder whether this concern also helped make him what he was, a largely independent thinker in a professional society where it was not easy to avoid being drawn into loyalty to one wing or the other. Perhaps the over-mothering of all those women in his childhood, at least as he experienced it, and the all too rich goodness of his family home (as Clare Winnicott suggests) made him reluctant to be put in that position again, preferring instead to become the nurturing figure for others, caring for his dependent wishes in them.

In 1914 Winnicott went up to Jesus College, Cambridge, to read biology, spending part of his time there helping in the military hospitals set up in some of the Cambridge colleges. Many of his friends entered the army, although as a medical student he was exempt. Clare Winnicott comments that because many of his close friends were killed in the war, 'always he felt a responsibility to live for those who died, as well as for himself' (Grolnick et al., 1978: 27). In his few pages of autobiography Winnicott wrote, 'I have never been free from the feeling that my being alive is a facet of some other thing of which their deaths can be seen as other facets: some huge crystal, a body with integrity and shape intrinsical to it' (quoted in Grolnick et al., 1978: 20). In November 1917, as was appropriate for a son of Plymouth, he himself joined up in the Royal Navy as a surgeon probationer, serving on a destroyer until the end of the war. (Masud Khan again writes mistakenly that he joined the army – Clancier and Kalmanovitch, 1987: xvi – and in Rudnytsky, 1991: 180, clearly he has Winnicott's religious upbringing wrong too.) Given the relatively short period of his studies to date it is scarcely surprising that Winnicott felt he knew nothing about medicine. Fortunately there was a medical orderly on board whom he could rely on, and who taught him. Clare Winnicott quotes the young Donald as writing back home to his mother, saying, 'I'm only here so that the men can write home and tell their mothers that there's a doctor on board.' Perhaps, as Neve suggests (Rudnytsky, 1991: 189), Winnicott was even then a comforting object. This period of his life was significant in other ways: he saw enemy action, witnessed death at first hand, and had to take action for himself. But he also had free time in which to read, including novels, particularly those of Henry James. He remained an avid reader – in fact he had read aloud to boys in his dormitory at school, and later in his life he used to read aloud to Clare. 'There was always a book on the go,' she comments (Rudnytsky, 1991: 189).

In 1918 Winnicott went straight to St Bartholomew's Hospital in London to continue his study of medicine, qualifying in 1920. There he came under the influence of Lord Horder. Watching him at work, Winnicott learned from him how important (and indeed how fascinating) it was to let people talk about themselves. Thomas Horder said to Winnicott, 'Listen to your patient. Don't go in with your wonderful knowledge and apply it all. Just listen. They tell you quite a lot of things. You'll learn a lot if you listen' (Rudnytsky, 1991: 189). To listen that carefully to the patient was, of course, highly unusual for a consultant and remains just as rare a quality in professionals today.

While Winnicott was a medical student he could not recall his dreams, although it is not clear why this bothered him. He looked for a book to help him and came upon one by Freud's Swiss friend Pfister. It led him in turn to Freud and to *The Interpretation of Dreams*. Freud's work was, of course, less widely known at that time, and in any case, as Winnicott once said, 'I was unaware when I was at school that these books were already written, and I doubt if I was ready for them then' (1957: 130). In a letter to his sister Violet, dated 15 November 1919, we can see his uncritical enthusiasm for this new-found subject. In it he explains to her what psychoanalysis is and how it differs from hypnosis by going to the root of the matter. He takes her through the divisions of the mind, crudely explains instinct theory, and confidently tells how Freud's methods can cure disorders of the mind: 'The patient is amazed to find his curious behaviour explained and the cause brought into consciousness.' Optimistically he clearly believes that 'he is then able to bring his own will into the battle and his will is given a fair chance'. The letter shows a simplistic understanding of what he acknowledges to be an 'astoundingly controversial' set of axioms. What pervades the writing is his desire to explain it all to her – perhaps as with reading books to others he has to communicate his own enthusiasm – and he writes somewhat prophetically: 'If there is anything which is not completely simple for anyone to understand I want you to tell me because I am now practising so that one day I shall be able to help introduce the subject to English people so that who runs may read' (Rodman, 1987: 2 – we note the Biblical quotation that concludes this sentence).

Finding the Way: Career, Analysis and Marriage

In 1923 Winnicott became physician to the Paddington Green Children's Hospital and Queen Elizabeth's Hospital, Hackney, a post he held for forty years. Clare Winnicott thought that he began to specialize in paediatrics because he wanted to stay in London in order to go into personal analysis. He also acquired rooms in the Harley Street area and set up a private practice, seeing some of the mothers and children from his hospital practice there too, when they were cases in which he was particularly interested. Winnicott's career as a paediatrician was marked by his care for ordinary families – not just the more privileged whom he might see in his private analytic practice, and who tend to be the ones who are described in his more extended case studies (*The Piggle*, 1980, and the doctor in *Holding and Interpretation*, 1989a). By the time he retired Winnicott had worked with over 60,000 cases in his three clinics. The districts he covered included many poor families, whom he also visited in their own homes – all of which surely gave both his psychoanalytic practice and his theoretical formulations quite a different perspective from that which might come from private practice alone.

He clearly had a way with children, although (or might it be partly *because*?) he had none of his own. His ability to engage with children will be made clear in the description of his practice in Chapter 3. Clare describes one detail, which does not appear in his own work, that he tried

> to round off and make significant a child's visit to him by giving the child something to take away which could afterwards be used and/or destroyed or thrown away. He would quickly reach for a piece of paper and fold it into some shape, usually a dart or a fan, which he might play with for a moment and then give to the child as he said goodbye. I never saw this gesture refused by any child. (Grolnick et al., 1978: 29)

This personal gift for working with children appears to have been a family trait, since his eldest sister is described as having had children come to visit her still in her nineties, and his middle sister ran a Brownie pack for many years.

A letter looking back on those years provides a window on to his attitude as a doctor. At one stage he had become entitled to beds in the hospital – an exciting opportunity because it brought status with it. 'Having beds means that one has arrived.' But Winnicott refused the step up:

> I said to myself: the distress of babies and small children in a hospital ward, even a very nice one, adds up to something terrific. Going into the

wards disturbs me very much. If I become an inpatient doctor I shall develop the capacity not to be disturbed by the distress of the children, otherwise I shall not be able to be an effective doctor. I will therefore concentrate on my O.P. [outpatient] work and avoid becoming callous in order to be efficient. (Rodman, 1987: 168)

The year 1923 was one which saw a number of beginnings for Winnicott – firstly, though not necessarily in order of importance to him, the appointments that started his career as a child physician, embracing paediatrics and child psychiatry; secondly entering personal analysis with James Strachey; thirdly his marriage with Alice Taylor, described by Phillips (1988) as a potter – although Masud Khan writes of her briefly and almost dismissively as a 'beautiful operatic singer', who 'went mad and taking care of her took all his youth' (Clancier and Kalmanovitch, 1987: xvi). It is interesting that all the short accounts of Winnicott's life scarcely mention this first marriage, which lasted for over 25 years. There is a reference in Clare's memoir to 'girlfriends' amongst friends of his sisters, and at Cambridge, and coming to 'the brink of marriage more than once' (Grolnick et al., 1978: 27-8). But the literature is dominated, at least in respect of Winnicott's intimate relationships, by the second marriage to Clare Britton. It is difficult, when Clare Winnicott (as she became) is the source of so much of the infor-mation in print about her husband's early life, work and interests, to be sure just how much the picture we have is complete, especially when so central an area as a marriage is given little or no attention.

We have to glean some of the missing information about this relationship from strange places. Donald and Alice Winnicott are referred to with some frequency, although mainly in passing, in Marion Milner's case study *In The Hands of the Living God* (1969). Her patient, Susan, had been found in a hospital for nervous diseases by a Mrs X, who 'had been visiting there and had become interested in this girl and had invited her to come and live with them' (Milner, 1969: 3). We now know that this Mrs X and her husband Mr X – 'a man of independent means, who was interested in problems to do with mental health', and who asked Marion Milner to undertake the analysis with Susan – were none other than the Winnicotts. This is surprising, because Winnicott not only writes the preface but is also separately referred to by name within the book as providing medical cover for Milner, who was a lay analyst. It is Judith Hughes who clarifies the identity of Mr and Mrs X (1989: 202), revealed to her by Marion Milner in a letter in 1986.

This first marriage ended in 1949. Winnicott's father had died, aged 93, on the last day of 1948 (his mother had died in 1925): the death of a parent as a trigger for separation and divorce is not unusual. It was also at this time that Winnicott had his first coronary. The ending of the marriage seems to have precipitated a regression in Milner's patient, who became 'very paranoid about Mr X, again insisting that he broke the marriage deliberately in order to "bitch her up"' (Milner, 1969: 113). Margaret Little, in analysis with Winnicott throughout this time, also describes how Winnicott told her about the divorce and coming remarriage, 'lest I should hear of it elsewhere or read it in the press'. She saw Winnicott's second coronary and his obvious depression as resulting from 'his distress about the question of breaking up his first marriage' (Little, 1990: 54–5). This is one of the few references to Winnicott having other than the most positive feelings – a necessary counter-balance to the one-sided picture that his second wife has bequeathed us.

The third major event of 1923 was the start of Winnicott's ten-year analysis with James Strachey – Strachey himself had been analysed by Freud, and was to become one of Freud's principal English translators. Winnicott's apparent motive in seeking therapy, in addition to his intellectual interest in the subject, was his description of himself as 'a rather inhibited young man asking whether anything could be done about it' (Hughes, 1989: 19). Of this analysis we obviously know only a small part. Winnicott wrote of Strachey that he 'had one thing quite clear in his mind as a result of his visit to Freud: that a process develops in the patient, and that what transpires cannot be produced but it can be made use of . . . It is my experience of analysis at the hand of Strachey that has made me suspicious of descriptions of interpretative work in analysis which seem to give credit to the interpretations for all that happens, as if the process in the patient had got lost sight of' (1969: 129). In a letter to Ernest Jones in 1952 Winnicott looked back on that analysis: 'Strachey made practically no mistakes and he adhered to a classical technique in a cold-blooded way for which I have always been grateful' although he said 'two or three things that were not interpretations at a time when interpretation was needed' (Rodman, 1987: 33). One of these was that Winnicott did not read enough Freud, which Winnicott subsequently saw was the result of an inhibition against reading Freud. In a letter to Strachey in 1951 he writes, 'You will be relieved to hear that I have done quite a bit of psychoanalytical reading, thanks to having been ill twice' (Rodman, 1987: 24). The published correspondence between James and Alix Strachey, at the time breaking confidentiality, reveals a few indiscreet details about the analysis: James refers at one point to 'poor little Winnie [suggesting] today that perhaps he pumped (urinated) over his ma at the moment of his birth'; and Alix appears to suggest that for Winnicott to end analysis he would perhaps need to 'f–ck his wife all of a sudden' (Meisel and Kendrick, 1985: 115, 166).

The Politics of Psychoanalysis

Winnicott was not accepted as a candidate for training within the British Psycho-Analytical Society until 1927. He qualified as an adult psychoanalyst in 1934, and as a child psychoanalyst in 1935, reading his paper 'The Manic Defence' (1975: 129–44) as the final part of the requirements for full membership. As Ernest Jones writes in a letter to Freud in 1937, Winnicott was the society's only male child analyst (Paskauskas, 1993: 755); and in addition, as Winnicott writes, 'at that time no other analyst was also a paediatrician so for two or three decades I was an isolated phenomenon' (1965b: 172). Winnicott recalls that in the course of his analysis, Strachey told him about Melanie Klein, which later led to Winnicott being supervised by her. He also had a second personal analysis from 1933 to 1938 with Joan Riviere, another of Freud's analysands but also one of Mrs Klein's most fervent supporters. Winnicott therefore became identified initially, although only until the mid-1940s, as a Kleinian. For readers unfamiliar with the politics of British psychoanalysis, these terms and their background must be explained.

After a shaky start, partly due to the controversy surrounding Freud's theories about infantile sexuality, psychoanalysis began to develop in a number of major centres. Not surprisingly, in the first two decades of the twentieth century Vienna and Berlin were the major psychoanalytic societies, with separate developments in Hungary, Switzerland, Italy, the United States and Canada. A London society proved abortive, and it was not until 1919 that the British Psycho-Analytical Society was formed, led for many years by the energetic Ernest Jones, one of Freud's most enthusiastic disciples and later his first major biographer. During the 1920s the practice of child analysis was systematically developed independently in Berlin by Melanie Klein, and in Vienna by Freud's daughter Anna. Melanie Klein came to London in 1926 at the invitation of Ernest Jones to analyse Jones's wife and two children. In London she found ready acceptance for her ideas, which borrowed from Freud's, and indeed were felt by her and her supporters to be the natural development of Freud's ideas, but which to others appeared to diverge significantly from Freud: for example, she emphasized the innate over and above the environment; she gave more substance to the reality of fantasy than to external reality; she wished to work with the child without the parents; she interpreted negative feelings towards the therapist

The life of D. W. Winnicott 15

from the start; and she placed the origins of the Oedipus complex in the first year of life.

Melanie Klein's ideas are highly relevant to an understanding of the way Winnicott developed his own thinking (see the companion volume in this series on *Melanie Klein*, Segal, 1992). Although he was her student (he was in supervision with Mrs Klein for six years from 1935–41), they each brought to the relationship particular strengths – Winnicott was already a careful observer of mothers and children and an experienced paediatrician, even if he was a student psychoanalyst when he first encountered her. He had some of the same doubts she had about tracing everything to the Oedipus complex at the age of about four or five; 'children who became disturbed . . . showed difficulties in their emotional development in infancy, even as babies' (1965b: 172). He recognized Mrs Klein as making 'the most vigorous attempt to study the earliest processes of the developing human infant apart from the study of child-care' (the latter his own field of expertise) (1965b: 126). Rodman mentions that 'in the early days, she wrote him long, affectionate letters' (1987: xx). Winnicott had wanted analysis with her, but she for her part wanted him to analyse her son under her supervision. He undertook the analysis, although not under her supervision.

The influence of Klein on Winnicott is examined in rather more detail in Chapter 2. For the present it is sufficient to remember that it was Mrs Klein and her growing number of followers who began to dominate the British Psycho-Analytical Society in the 1930s. But in 1938, following high-level diplomatic negotiations in which Ernest Jones was once again involved, Freud and his daughter Anna were brought to London out of Nazi-occupied Vienna. According to Anna Freud, Winnicott was 'the only member of the British Society who called at their Maresfield Gardens home to ask if they were all right' (Rodman, 1987: xix), although there is no other record of Winnicott ever meeting Freud himself, and Rodman suggests that the letters between Miss Freud and Winnicott 'attest to a formal distance' between them (1987: xix). Following Sigmund Freud's death in 1939 the divisions present in the British Psycho-Analytical Society flared up. Controversy raged over whether Melanie Klein's ideas were a deviation from the true course of psychoanalysis. A letter from Winnicott's former analyst James Strachey to the chairman of the training committee in 1940 describes the situation well:

> The trouble seems to me to be extremism, on both sides. My own view is that Mrs K. has made some highly important contributions to PA

[psychoanalysis], but that it's absurd to make out (a) that they cover the whole subject or (b) that their validity is axiomatic. On the other hand I think it's equally ludicrous for Miss F. to maintain that PA is a Game Reserve belonging to the F. family and that Mrs K's ideas are totally subversive. These attitudes on both sides are of course purely religious and the very antithesis of science. (King and Steiner, 1991: 33)

In the light of these remarks it may appear odd that the meetings that were arranged to examine the differences were known as 'discussions of scientific controversies'. The more common term, 'the controversial discussions', is less pretentious. Winnicott was an important member of the Kleinian group, since he had been named by Mrs Klein as one of five Kleinian training analysts. Despite being out of London in connection with his work with children evacuated from the Blitz, he attended all the extraordinary business meetings of the Society and all but one of the special scientific meetings, taking an active part in the discussions. But, perhaps not surprisingly for one who came from an already independent religious tradition, and for one whose first analyst was also clearly sceptical about such a feud, he was in fact an individualist. According to a letter to one of her supporters, Mrs Klein experienced problems with him 'because he did not give her his contributions early enough for her or the group to vet them, and he made a number of "blunders"' (King and Steiner, 1991: xxiv). In the end, by 1945, the pragmatic and perhaps typically British solution to the controversy was the formation of two paths of training within the Society, and in effect three groups of practitioners. Course A students followed a training which included Kleinian as well as Freudian ideas about technique; course B students undertook a course in line with Freudian technique alone. Other lectures were in common. But in their supervision, both course A and course B students were required, where they had had a supervisor from their own group in the first instance, to have a second supervisor chosen from a third independent group. The effect of this, even though later the requirement for a second supervisor was dropped, was to make analysts identify either with group A (the Kleinians), group B (the Freudians) or a third 'middle group'. Faced during these discussions with a demand by Mrs Klein on his loyalty perhaps too great for his independent spirit to accept, and also with what might possibly have felt to Winnicott to be a repeat of his childhood experience of 'too many mothers', he became identified with the analysts in the 'middle group', such as Michael Balint, W. R. D. Fairbairn, Marion Milner, and later Charles Rycroft, Masud Khan, Peter Lomas – some of whom subsequently left the Society altogether (see Rayner, 1990 for a study of the main independent writers).

As has been indicated already, during the period of these wartime discussions, Winnicott became psychiatric consultant to the Government Evacuation Scheme in Oxfordshire, and worked at this time with psychiatric social workers such as Clare Britton, whom he was later to marry in 1951 after his divorce. Madeleine Davis comments that the experience of the evacuation scheme enabled Winnicott to bring together the impact of the environment as well as of inner reality in his theory, thus distinguishing him further from Mrs Klein's position (1981: 183). His findings during the war confirmed the conclusions of John Bowlby's study of stealing and of a child's separation from mother. Winnicott also came to see the value of many factors in therapy other than interpretation. Recalling his visits to a hostel in Bicester, he self-mockingly contrasts his own 'smashing interpretations based on deep insight' with what he quickly learned, that 'therapy was being done in the institution, by the walls and the roof; by the glass conservatory which provided a target for bricks . . . by the cook, by the regularity of arrival of food on the table' (1984: 221). This was one of the knocks to his training, 'that there is something about psychotherapy which is not to be described in terms of making the right interpretation at the right moment' (1984: 222).

Following the war, Winnicott played a central part in the activities of the British Psycho-Analytical Society. He was physician in charge of the Child Department of the Institute of Psycho-Analysis for 25 years. His letters reveal continuing concern with the sniping that continued to take place between the Freudians and the Kleinians. In one, written in 1954 when he was training secretary, he wrote to both Miss Freud and Mrs Klein, concerned about the continuation of the two groupings, which had in his opinion ceased to serve their original purpose ten years before. He foresaw that the death of either of these women would lead to the hardening of rigid groupings, and this appalled him. 'I consider it to be of absolutely vital importance to the future of the Society that both of yourselves shall break up the groupings in so far as they are official. No one can break them up except yourselves and you can only do this while you are alive' (Rodman, 1987: 73). In an earlier letter in 1952 to Mrs Klein alone, Winnicott sets out his concerns even more strongly. He begins by acknowledging the great contribution she has made, while recognizing that he can himself be seen as annoying because he has 'ideas that are personal and original'. What he was looking for in a paper he had delivered, he says, was a response from her group to his gesture of an attempted move in their direction. In an enigmatic gloss upon his own experience of analysis he goes on: 'I think that I was wanting something which I have no right to expect from your group, and it is really of the nature of a therapeutic act, something which I could not get in either of my two long analyses, although I got so much else.' Referring to his analysis with Mrs Riviere, he says 'that it was just exactly here that her analysis failed me'. Winnicott is deeply concerned that Mrs Klein's insistence that only her own 'language shall be used for the statement of other people's discoveries' will make her language a dead one. He pleads with her as 'the only one who can destroy this language called the Kleinian doctrine and Kleinism'. In a graphic image of one member's paper in which he 'simply bandied about a lot of that which has now come to be known as Kleinian stuff without giving any impression of having an appreciation of the processes personal to the patient', Winnicott says 'that if he were growing a daffodil he would think that he was making the daffodil out of the bulb, instead of enabling the bulb to develop into a daffodil by good enough nurture' (Rodman, 1987: 33–7).

Such internal debates can seem confusing to the outsider. But there are other confusions in the tight world of psychoanalysis, which impinge to some extent on the study of one who challenged some of the analytic conventions in his technique. Melanie Klein, for example, also analysed Winnicott's second wife, Clare. Reference has already been made to Winnicott treating Mrs Klein's son, as indeed he treated Ernest Jones's daughter. Masud Khan, who edited all Winnicott's papers between 1950 and 1970, and every book published during Winnicott's life time, was also analysed by him for ten years, and so was Masud Khan's wife. We wonder what such inter-relationships do both for personal analyses and also for outside relations. We must also wonder what the effect was on Marion Milner's patient Susan, when Winnicott's wife found her, when he referred her, when the Winnicotts had her living in their home, and through all this time were friends and colleagues of her analyst. These examples of confusing boundary issues, and potentially crossed wires, are perhaps inevitable in what is in fact a relatively small professional community. Nonetheless it is an influential community that at times has been deeply critical of what it sees as less than ideal standards in the wider field of counselling and therapy.

In addition to serving as training secretary and scientific secretary, Winnicott was president of the British Psycho-Analytical Society for two terms (1956–9, 1965–8). He keenly attended many of the fortnightly meetings of the Institute, and some of his letters show that he was not slow to write soon afterwards to those who had delivered papers. As Lomas comments, in a review of the Winnicott correspondence:

He appears to have little doubt about his own views and few inhibitions in criticizing those of others . . . These letters can seldom have brought comfort to their recipients. There must be many an analyst who, after breakfasting with one of Winnicott's letters, felt more inclined to go back to bed rather than to face his patients. (1987b: 798)

For example, in 1952 he writes to Hanna Segal: 'I do think that just at times for a few minutes you are tremendously cocksure of yourself, and if you happen to be speaking just then it shows . . . The fact is that you are capable of failing just as other analysts are . . . I am concerned that you shall not spoil it all by getting into some sort of ugly state in which you are sitting perched up on top of a Mount Everest of an internalized good breast' (Rodman, 1987: 26). The delightful style shows that Winnicott was not averse himself to cock-shying the apparently cocksure, and indicates how he could be, in the words of one of his erstwhile protégés, 'engaging, enjoyable, very alive, charming, wise, but patronising, subtly controlling and keen for prominence' (personal communication).

Winnicott may have felt like a cock-shy himself when he delivered his paper 'The Use of an Object' to the New York Psychoanalytic Society in 1968, and had it knocked about by three discussants. He is described as responding 'in a charming and whimsical fashion' (but was this defensive?) that his concept was 'torn to pieces and that he would be happy to give it up' (Rudnytsky, 1991: 105). That same year in York (England) Winnicott received the acclaim of fellow paediatricians with the award of James Spence Medal for Paediatrics; but in New York he regarded his paper as a failure. Shortly afterwards he had a major heart attack, but whether this was due to the critical reception can only be speculation. In his own letters to speakers and on the evening in question, Winnicott's concern was for intellectual exchange rather than personal rancour. But Lomas, who admires 'the integrity, passion, intelligence and common sense' in the letter, also feels 'disquiet at their narcissism' (1987: 798). Was the criticism in New York too strong a narcissistic wound?

'Not Less than Everything'

As Davis comments, 'the quarter century from 1945 until Winnicott's death saw an almost incredible surge of activity' (Davis and Wallbridge, 1981: 185). Winnicott achieved considerable prominence outside psychoanalytic circles. He was at various times chairman of the Medical Section of the British Psychological Society, president of the Paediatric Section of the Royal Society of Medicine, president of the Association of Child Psychology and Psychiatry. He was a member of UNESCO and WHO study groups. His published correspondence shows a lively interest in political debate; it was not just to colleagues but elsewhere that he fired off letters: to *The Times*, to medical journals, to Lord Beveridge – even, before the Second World War, to the Prime Minister's wife, not believing the Prime Minister would have time to read his letter! His letters comment on a variety of topics about which he had passionate convictions, such as his opposition to anti-Semitism, electro-convulsive therapy or leucotomy. They were not always liberal views. He criticized sponsored television; and the setting up of the National Health Service he described as 'the nationalisation of the medical profession'. He even recorded his disagreement with sexually accurate dolls, writing, 'the logical conclusion would be to make a teddy bear which really bites if you tease it' (Rodman, 1987: 4, 6–9, 14–15, 15–16, 76–7).

Winnicott was in great demand as a lecturer and enjoyed visiting non-psychoanalytic groups. He turned his attention to many topics, although he was largely concerned with the application of psycho-analysis to other professional settings – social workers, midwives, clergy, teachers, student health physicians and nurses, the Nursery School Association, Christian Teamwork, the Oxford University Scientific Society. *Home Is Where We Start From* (1986) consists of many such papers on subjects that range from 'Psychoanalysis and Science: Friends or Relations?' to 'This Feminism', 'The Pill and the Moon' and 'The Place of the Monarchy'. Some of those who heard him speak clearly remember the occasion, but not all appear to have found him a particularly impressive speaker. One psychiatric social work student at the London School of Economics found his lectures there difficult to understand, although his drawings of the relation between the baby and the breast were impressed upon her memory (the annual lectures, with some of the drawings, appear in *Human Nature*, 1988b). Others have commented on his spontaneity, recalling him (for example) as breaking into singing Bach to illus-trate a point, or as a 'jack-in-a-box . . . sitting on the back row . . . like some disjointed marionette . . . [he] unwound like a spring' and brought back to life an audience of which he was a member (Clancier and Kalmanovitch, 1987: xi).

Perhaps the widest audience and best known of Winnicott's work came with his series of broadcast talks on BBC Radio, some given during the Second World War but most in the second half of the 1940s. Here he showed again his enthusiasm for communicating 'for anyone to understand', as he had wished in his 1919 letter to his sister. The printed text demonstrates beyond doubt his ability to reach to the heart of the relationship between mother and baby, as well as to reach the minds of parents and others who are not otherwise used to assimilating psychoanalytic concepts – and who indeed may not even have realized that it is such concepts they have digested. There is no particular sales talk in them for partisan ideas. The editor of many of the posthumous publications writes: 'I doubt if anyone has spoken with such immediacy about how ordinary parents and their babies and children actually behave and feel towards each other' (Davis and Wallbridge, 1981: 187). Published first in 1957 in two volumes, with a few other papers, they were printed together (in the main) in *The Child, the Family and the Outside World* in 1964. This paperback book sold 50,000 copies in its first three years and was reprinted four times before its author died in 1971. It remains in print and continues to sell well.

Rodman comments that 'many books flowed from his pen' (1987: xvi). It may appear that this is the case, although in fact Winnicott wrote mostly papers and case notes, and it is these that have been collected into books, nearly always edited by others. The majority of the more than 100 lectures and papers have appeared in print since his death. As will become clear both in the exposition of his theory (Chapter 2) and in the critique of him (Chapter 4), it is important to acknowledge that he was essentially a prolific writer of short papers, not an author of extensively argued books. There is very little sign, except perhaps in the lecture notes published in *Human Nature* (1988b), of any attempt to present an extended theory put together as a coherent whole. It is as if Winnicott's spontaneity, energy and enthusiasm for sharing his ideas with others results in relatively short bursts of work, written either in response to a request to speak or from material coming out of his practice, but not necessarily cross-referring to other parts of the theoretical framework. It is perhaps also significant, as I suggested in the introduction to this chapter, that Winnicott is remembered much more for catch-phrases such as 'the good-enough mother' and 'the transitional object', as well as for the personal qualities illustrated in his therapeutic manner, than he is for any major theoretical model.

Nevertheless these phrases that are familiar to many counsellors and therapists represent the distillation of a prodigious output. That he produced so much can perhaps be understood through Simone Decobert's interpretation of his self-confidence

> that characterizes certain discoverers, who are convinced that they have nothing to lose by expounding their observations and hypotheses in all honesty: he also possessed that other kind of self-confidence, which, as Freud said, characterizes the child who knows that he was his parents' favourite, especially his mother's favourite. (Clancier and Kalmanovitch, 1987: xii)

Superlatives feature indeed throughout the literature about Winnicott's life, whether in recording the huge number of cases he saw, or in the glowing descriptions given of his personal qualities. Masud Khan concludes his introduction to the 1975 edition of *Through Paediatrics to Psycho-Analysis* with the words 'Winnicott was one such the like of whom I shall not meet again' (1975: xxxxviii). His widow Clare, upon whose memoir and memories we have to depend for much of our information about his private and social life, presents a picture which at times saturates us with his energy and abilities. Such descriptions highlight the vast amount that Winnicott packed into his life. Yet he appears not to have been what would now be called a workaholic. His schedule allowed space for many leisure interests, which Clare Winnicott lists, as if his spare time was also filled with reading, playing the piano, watching television, enjoying art and poetry, and just sitting, as he and Clare used to, on the floor.

From her memoir we gather that at Cambridge Winnicott was a popular figure whose room was a meeting place. At medical school he 'soaked himself in medicine and fully committed himself to the whole experience' including writing for the hospital magazine, singing, dancing, skiing, and 'hurrying off at the last minute to hear operas for the first time' (Grolnick et al., 1978: 27). In his workplace he was visited by 'many colleagues from all over the world'. In his leisure time he loved reading: mostly biographies, but he also liked Virginia Woolf, and writing in the style of 'the stream of consciousness'. He loved music and would 'rush up and play the piano between patients' (Rudnytsky, 1991: 190), and at the end of the day would play 'a musical outburst fortissimo'. Particularly towards the end of his life, Clare goes on to describe in her interview with Neve (Rudnytsky, 1991: 192), Winnicott was always listening to the late Beethoven quartets, fascinated by them and their structure. He loved Bach, which he could play without sheet music. He also 'greatly enjoyed the Beatles and bought all their recordings' (Grolnick et al., 1978: 30). He enjoyed going to see pictures, preferring classical painting to modernism.

Clare Winnicott stresses his – and indeed their – ability to *play*, using a central term that of course featured in so much of his writing and in his professional work with children. She recalls that a visitor to their house said to her, 'You and Donald play, don't you?' This surprised her, because she had not thought of it in that way. Her guest went on, 'Oh yes you do. You play with me. You play with all kinds of things. My wife and I, we don't play.' Clare realized then that they played with their furniture, with books, with reading, with going out (Rudnytsky, 1991: 182). Elsewhere she writes, 'We played with things – our possessions – rearranging, acquiring, and discarding according to our mood. We played with ideas, tossing them at random with the freedom of knowing that we need not agree, and that we were strong enough not to be hurt by each other . . . we were operating in the play area where everything is permissible' (Grolnick et al., 1978: 29). Saturdays were always set aside for play, with nothing done by either of them except enjoying themselves, although sometimes they worked on Sundays (Grolnick et al., 1978: 27–8).

The sense of play and fun in Winnicott is illustrated in his enjoyment of 'rolling in the grass' and riding his bicycle down Haverstock Hill in Hampstead, London, with his feet on the handlebars. Clare Winnicott tells how a policeman stopped him and commented on the example an old man like him was setting everybody. She also remembered him driving his car with his head through the roof and a walking stick on the accelerator. 'He'd try anything. He was the most spontaneous thing that ever lived' (Rudnytsky, 1991: 193). Whether or not such antics in public are as amusing as she would have us believe perhaps needs considering. The policeman may have been right: there are some boundaries the crossing of which can be dangerous to others. Clare gives no sense of this, and, following the lead of her memories, none of the biographical material does either. But some readers may wonder at this point, if they have not already wondered before, whether what Clare Winnicott has created is more a hagiography than an introduction to a biography.

She refers in print to the negative side of her husband only once, claiming that he showed his anger towards her when she had hurt herself or was ill. 'He hated to have me as a patient, and not as his wife and playmate' (Grolnick et al., 1978: 31). One explanation for this anger with illness in her occurs in the next paragraph of Clare's reflection on their relationship, where she quotes one of Donald's letters to her, written before they married, in which he appears to make a close link between his love for Clare and his love for his sister's doll – the implication in his letter being that Clare is a type of transitional object for him. This is a rare glimpse in her account of another side to Winnicott, one which begins to flesh him out and perhaps even flush him out from the eulogy which otherwise serves to hide the weaknesses and vulnerability which surely must have been his, as much as they are part of each of us. Margaret Little's conclusion is more rounded: 'As with any outstanding personality it is only too easy to idealize or to denigrate D. W., to think of him as "charismatic" or a "cult figure", but to do either is to *dehumanize* him, to cling to phantasy and misconception' (1990: 70, her emphasis).

'He wanted to live', comments Clare Winnicott, confirming the aptness of the intended title of his autobiography, that was to be called *Not Less than Everything*, a quotation from T. S. Eliot. It opens with the words: 'Prayer: Oh God, may I be alive when I die' (Rudnytsky, 1991: 193). But beneath the seamless robe which she weaves around his life and around his relationship with her – clearly an intense and inspirational one for them both, with Clare like a Beatrice to his Dante – there remain questions. With only a few pages of his intended autobiography and in the absence of a definitive biography, we might ask whether it is really true that in the picture of Winnicott that is presented a generation after his death we have 'not less than everything'?

Winnicott's life was packed. His work load was huge. He held down a public service consultancy together with a private practice, and with all that his increasing importance as a speaker and an expert on child care brought with it. As I have already described, even his leisure time is portrayed as full of stimulating appreciation of music, art, literature, sport and the modern media. In much of his work Winnicott gave added meaning to the 'spaces in between'. But for one who wrote, as I mentioned earlier, 'that gaps in knowledge and understanding need not scare me' (1957: 129), I find myself wondering what the gaps were in him, which the next generation has not yet been allowed to see. His energy, his enthusiasm, his originality, his wit and his obvious loving nature – all these are well painted in what we learn of him. But it is natural that we should also ask what else was going on in him which the seductively attractive side of him might mask. What was that first marriage like? What did it mean to him not to have children? Where were the sadness, the emptiness and all those other feelings which we would expect in 'not less than everything'? He shows no anxiety about allowing space for his patients, as the more detailed description of his work in Chapter 3 shows. But was he in some way afraid of the space which his active life and leisure seems continually to have filled?

Look a little closer, and there is another side to the sanitized picture which his widow portrays. For example, towards the end of his life he suffered a series of coronaries. Despite six such attacks, he kept going, not stopping himself from doing anything. Was that an unwillingness to pause and allow himself space, for fear of what would then enter it? Again, when he was cutting a tree in his West country home, his wife thought he was crazy – given his heart condition – to be lopping the top off it because it spoiled the view. But she thought next that it was his life, and he had to live it. Again we might ask, behind the affection of her remark, did she not have a right to question his concern for her? Did all this activity have to centre round him, or might he have taken care of himself at that point for her sake as well? And finally, because it must await a more definite and searching life for the other side of the picture to be examined, even in that memorable phrase 'May I be alive when I die' might we detect a haunting fear of not being in control, seen most obviously in that decision to enter medicine to avoid having to 'depend on doctors if I damaged myself or became ill'?

In fact, as Clare Winnicott tells us, his last day, 25 January 1971, was like that. They were in their London home, listening to music when Clare spotted a comic film on the television. He and Clare had watched the film about old cars, which he had described as a 'happy-making film', after which they both went to sleep on the floor. Earlier in the day Clare recalls that she had looked at him, and thought that if she really loved him she would not want him to go on much longer. When she awoke from her own sleep, he had died in his (Rudnytsky, 1991: 192-3).

The two publications that were in press at the time, *Playing and Reality* and *Therapeutic Consultations in Child Psychiatry*, were published that year. But Winnicott had left boxes of unpublished material and ring-binders full of letters. A few years after his death a committee was set up under the auspices of his widow to enable the best of his work to be brought to publication. Madeleine Davis, one of the principal editors of that material, writes: 'This was, in fact, in keeping with Winnicott's own wishes for he had himself planned to have more books published containing a mixture of unpublished papers and papers from journals and anthologies' (Davis and Wallbridge, 1981: 173). Further papers were found after Clare Winnicott's death in 1984. Madeleine Davis died in 1991, having brought most of the material to the point of publication. These and all his publications prior to his death are listed in the select bibliography of Winnicott's writing at the back of this volume. My examination of his theories and his practice in the next two chapters is drawn from these many papers, so full of ideas that sometimes challenge and nearly always refresh conventional therapeutic wisdom. Winnicott wrote for his own profession, but he also spoke to and wrote for those whose caring work takes the same lively interest he himself did in the practical relevance and straightforward communication of psychoanalytic ideas. His wit, his imagination, his careful and caring observation, his playfulness and gift for words, and his sense of the suggestiveness of paradox for the most part make reading him a pleasure.

In the memorial address honouring Winnicott, subsequently printed as the obituary in the *International Journal of Psycho-Analysis* (1971: 52, 3), his old friend and fellow paediatrician Peter

Tizard said that 'to say that he understood children would to me sound false and vaguely patronizing; it was rather that children understood him and that he was at one with them'. In the end this quality may be one of the factors that makes Winnicott such a popular figure amongst therapists and counsellors of different persuasions. It is not only that we feel he often understands us. It is also that for the most part we feel (even if in some respects this is bound to be illusory) that we understand him.

2
Major Contributions to Theory

The Influences on Winnicott's Thinking

There are a number of senses in which we can say that Winnicott was an original thinker. The first sense is the obvious one, that he must be credited with certain concepts and methods of practice that are clearly his own: the idea of the transitional object and transitional phenomena is one example of this. The squiggle game is another, even if quite independently Robert Hobson (1985) later used virtually the same technique. The second sense in which he is original is in his ability to adapt, and to make his own, concepts and aspects of clinical practice which others had pioneered. Here we could cite the significant shift he makes in Sigmund Freud's concept of illusion, so that it becomes in Winnicott a way of perceiving the present rather than, as in Freud, an indication of childlike wish-fulfilment; or Winnicott's adaptation of play therapy to include the spatula game in his clinical consultations with infants and mothers.

The third sense in which he is original would perhaps not always be acknowledged as such in academic circles, but nevertheless is an indication of an independent and creative mind: Winnicott normally worked out his ideas first for himself, and only then checked up to see who might have influenced him. His description of his method is found in a letter to David Rapaport: 'I am one of those people who feel compelled to work in my own way and to express myself in my own language first; by a struggle I sometimes come round to rewording what I am saying to bring it in line with other work, in which case I usually find that my own "original" ideas were not so original as I had to think when they were emerging. I suppose other people are like this too' (Rodman, 1987: 53–4). Elsewhere he prefaces one scientific paper with the caveat that 'I shall not first give an historical survey and show the development of my ideas from the theories of others, because my mind does not work that way. What happens is that I gather this and that, here and there, settle down to clinical experience, form my own theories, and then, last of all, interest myself to see where I stole what' (1975: 145). The academic world gives little credit to those whose contribution includes discovering for themselves that which others, unknown to them, have already anticipated – unless by some chance they happen to be the first to appear in print. Yet this third sense of originality, one which as Winnicott rightly surmises is common to many other people, is certainly not to be denigrated. In his case we have the added bonus that his way of putting what others may have similarly suggested is often refreshingly original.

As far as we can gather, Winnicott's principal method of working was to think through for himself the sense that he tried to make of his observations. He makes it clear that he does not mind whether or not he is being original. Just as he himself had no wish that others should follow in a 'Winnicottian' school, so too he normally does not appear to worry that he does not immediately fit into a Freudian or a Kleinian mould – these are the two major divisions within psychoanalysis that overshadowed the British Psycho-Analytical Society of which he was both a member and for many years an officer. In a lecture in the United States he said, 'I do not claim to be able to hand out the Kleinian view in a way that she would herself approve of . . . I believe my views began to separate out from hers . . . I have never been able to follow anyone else, not even Freud' (1965b: 176). What mattered more was that he could work out further for himself what he wished to understand. Perhaps this is why much of his writing has vitality, because his language, if sometimes technical (he was after all often writing for a particular professional audience), can also be extraordinarily ordinary. In a letter to Anna Freud he referred to himself and two other analysts: 'we are all trying to express the same things, only I have an irritating way of saying things in my own language instead of learning how to use the terms of psycho-analytic meta-psychology' (Rodman, 1987: 58).

It is this which is so attractive to the counsellor or therapist who is less conversant with, or even unsure about, the complex termin-ology that is indicative of much psychoanalytic writing, and that confines its use to a relatively narrow readership. Winnicott's capacity to convey his observations, observations that we too have made but have not yet fully registered, means that time and again in his writing the reader nods in assent, and smiles at the pleasure of recognizing the particular significance he gives to common experi-ence. The most obvious place where he writes in this way is in *The Child, the Family and the Outside World* (1964), where the reader (and originally the listener to his broadcasts) is introduced to what are in essence complex concepts about the processes of a child's thinking and fantasy. But never at any point does the reader feel that he or she has been lost in technical jargon: Winnicott's observations (even of internal processes) are usually well rooted in external signs. Even his more technical papers, although they draw upon psychoanalytic terminology, similarly provide enough instances of immediate recognition to make them in large measure accessible to a wide readership outside psychoanalysis itself.

In Winnicott's theoretical position there is a significant shift away from the father–child relationship to the nursing couple, from Oedipal issues to the formation of the self, from classical Freudian theory to his own version of object relations theory (the most significant of post-Freudian developments), from drive and instinct to need, and from an over-emphasis upon fantasy (Winnicott uses the conventional spelling rather than 'phantasy') to the centrality of the environmental provision. If these terms also appear technical, I explain them further below. The developmental sequence of the three stages of childhood is replaced by a concentration upon the tasks involved in the growth towards maturity.

As he makes clear, Winnicott does not deny that he has a debt to others; neither does he ever lay claim to complete originality. It is rather that precedence does not appear to interest him, as for example it haunted Freud. Nevertheless it is appropriate to look both for the influence upon him and the parallels in his writing, particularly with reference to the key concepts of Sigmund Freud and Melanie Klein, perhaps the two most significant figures for psychoanalytic thought and practice. With the exception of one paper devoted purely to Klein, in his collections of papers from 1957 onwards (1965a; 1965b; 1971a) Winnicott makes surprisingly little reference to her. He refers to Sigmund Freud a little more. Nevertheless we have to remember that even when he does not make direct references, some of the key ideas of both Freud and Klein pervade his own thinking – the inner world and internal objects, the importance of phantasy, and instinctual gratification, to take just a few examples. Nor should we overlook that early and pervading impression that Darwin made upon him. But in the case of all three thinkers, Winnicott adapts his antecedents (as might be expected of a Darwinian) and provides a unique slant.

Taking these three influences in the chronological order of their impact upon him, Winnicott makes his own use of Darwinian theory. Darwin said that a species has to adapt to its environment, which it does through natural selection; those species that have adapted in a variety of ways stand the greater chance of survival, because there are more chances that a particular adaptation will suit its environment. As Phillips points out, Winnicott revises part of Darwin. Firstly he sees the baby's mother (who in the early weeks *is* of course the baby's environment) as having to adapt to the baby, as the baby is assisted in adapting to the wider environment beyond the mother. Phillips also observes that Winnicott 'reverses the Darwinian equation by suggesting that human development was an often ruthless struggle against compliance with the environment' (1988: 5). I examine this further below when discussing the concept of the true and the false (compliant) self.

Phillips further observes that Winnicott sometimes uses language less than carefully: 'the word "natural" . . . does a lot of devious work in Winnicott's writing' (1988: 4). He also with 'a certain disingenuousness . . . disguises his radical departures from Freud' (1988: 5). I recorded in Chapter 1 Winnicott's own reference to his later inhibition about reading much Freud. Although he admired Freud for his clarity of thinking, his ability to write, and the way in which he was not afraid to change his mind, not surprisingly he was also critical of him: 'I am a product of the Freudian or psychoanalytic school. This does not mean that I take for granted everything Freud said or wrote' (1965a: 21). He does not follow Freud's *emphasis* on the place of the father, on erotic sexuality, or upon the centrality of the Oedipus complex, although none of these is totally omitted from Winnicott's writing. He recognizes that Freud wrote for a particular age, and that he would have advanced his ideas with the growth of understanding of infancy. In a revision of his paper on birth memories, Winnicott comments that 'I think I can find everything that I have suggested somewhere in his [i.e. Freud's] writings' (1975: 174). Similarly in his paper on the spatula game (see also Chapter 3), he refers to Freud's parallel observation of his grandson dropping a cotton reel out of the pram, although he adds his own interpretation of what this might mean, that it is about playing with the idea of the temporary loss of mother (1975: 68).

Greenberg and Mitchell, in their comprehensive overview of object relations theory, observe that Winnicott provides a foundation for developmental theory that is 'radically different' from Freud and Klein, although he tries to preserve tradition 'in a curious fashion, largely by distorting it' (1983: 189). They provide several examples of the way in which he strikingly misreads Freud, despite taking 'great pains, at times involving elaborate and intricate argumentation, to proclaim himself at one with Freud in all respects' (1983: 205). They show this distortion in relation to Winnicott's understanding of Freud's position on narcissism, Oedipal guilt, and the false self. In the last case, for example, they demonstrate how Winnicott makes 'an extremely misleading parallel' (1983: 207). They similarly observe that while Winnicott openly departs from Klein 'on many issues, the treatment of Klein in his writing reflects a considerable effort to demonstrate his continuity with her views', although his 'alteration of Klein's formulations is much more covert' (1983: 203). What is difficult to know is how much pressure he felt under to make references to both Freud and Klein, and to the continuity of his own ideas in relation to them, because of the internal politics of psychoanalysis. At one time it was almost *de rigeur* to make 'credal statements' in order to be accepted. Much as Winnicott despised the in-fighting and rigid positions adopted by some members of the London society, he probably could not free himself entirely from running with the hare and hunting with the hounds if he wished his own contributions to be heard and discussed.

Since Winnicott was at an early formative stage supervised by Melanie Klein we might expect her influence to be extensive. Phillips asserts that 'his work cannot . . . be understood without reference to Klein' (1988: 9), particularly the foundations of the early years of infancy and childhood, the importance of the inner world, the power of phantasy, and the idea of primitive greed. Winnicott himself recalls how as a paediatrician he realized that the familiar 'Oedipus complex' explanation of the 1920s was not sufficient to explain the difficulties that could be seen in emotional development in infancy. In Klein he 'found an analyst who had a great deal to say about the anxieties that belong to infancy' (1965b: 173). In the paper that traces her contribution to psychoanalysis (and by implication her contribution to his own thinking and practice) he cites examples of what he got from her 'generous' teaching, such as the use of toys, playing as a way into a child's inner world, the connection between the mental mechanisms of introjection and the function of eating, projection, inner and outer worlds, the persecutory quality of internal objects, primitive defences, and reactive depression (1965b: 174–5). This is a considerable list. He valued too her understanding of the depressive position, although not the name she gave it. Neither did he like the term 'paranoid–schizoid', although he did not wish to ignore some of what she meant by this. He also learned from her about the capacity for concern (although he transformed her theory here), and the positive achievement of guilt.

Nevertheless there are major differences, such as his rejection of the idea of a death instinct (1965b: 191); and especially in the importance he attached to *actual* environmental provision, as opposed to her emphasis upon innate predisposition and fantasy. This is reflected not just in his practice as a child psychotherapist (in which parents have a very important part to play), but also in his theoretical framework, in which he assigns a vital role in development to the actual task of mothering. If this view appears to swing him in the direction of Anna Freud's position on child psychotherapy, I remind the reader that there was 'a formal distance' between them (Rodman, 1987: xix). Indeed, as he wrote in a letter in 1968, 'for a long time, as you know, I was not asked to do any teaching of psycho-analysis because neither Miss Freud nor Mrs Klein would use me or allow their students to come to me for regular teaching' (Rodman, 1987: 179).

British psychoanalysis developed politically into three groupings – the Freudians, the Kleinians and the independent or 'middle group'. Winnicott clearly must be placed in this last, alongside, although not always in agreement with, Fairbairn, Balint, Bowlby, Rycroft, Guntrip, and his own disciple Masud Khan. He is certainly on a par with the independent Scottish psychoanalyst Fairbairn, but easier to read (although sometimes Winnicott's apparent simplicity is deceptive); and he is probably more popular with the wider psychodynamic world. Winnicott was himself critical of Fairbairn's work. Greenberg and Mitchell describe both Klein and Fairbairn as 'system-builders. Each constructed a broad and novel vision of human experience and difficulties' (1983: 188). Winnicott they place with Guntrip as concerned more with single issues, presenting their contributions as 'circumscribed and limited'.

Phillips clearly would disagree since he describes Winnicott as developing a 'master-plot of human development that he worked on for over forty years' (1988: 2), although this is probably a rather too rounded way of describing it. Winnicott made little attempt to integrate his quarrying of numerous observations and ideas into a single edifice. Hardly any of his writing attempts to construct a clear theoretical structure, except the series of lectures which he was continually refining and which were published posthumously in *Human Nature* (1988b). Greenberg and Mitchell's description of Winnicott is both realistic and complimentary:

> The central themes are generally presented in the form of evocative paradoxes that entice the reader playfully. The arguments are more discursive than tightly reasoned . . . Harold Bloom has suggested that each major poet within the Western tradition distorts the vision of his most prominent predecessors to make room for his personal vision. Winnicott's manner of positioning his own innovative and important contributions vis-à-vis the psychoanalytic tradition suggests such a process. (1983: 189)

Rodman agrees. Winnicott, he suggests, did not need a convincing philosophical system, just as he found himself at one time, in his own words, 'absolutely unable to take part in a metapsychological discussion' (Rodman, 1987: 127). Rodman's description of him is delightful and unpretentious: 'Winnicott drops into our astonished midst like a parachutist who is entitled to be right where he is' (1987, xxix).

If there is not a definitive structure in Winnicott's theory, it is sufficient to form a sequence, as the subjects I deal with below indicate. There is of course a danger that in trying for clarity I make his thinking too neat, and to be too neat would be contrary to his way of working. In relation to the therapy session he wrote what surely must also be a warning to anyone trying to unravel his ideas: 'There is room for the idea of unrelated thought sequences which the analyst will do well to accept as such, not assuming the existence of a significant thread' (1971a: 54).

The sheer volume of his writing might at first suggest that it is an impossible task to encompass his position in one chapter – especially when there are already some fine summaries which are able to devote more space to his ideas than I have here. The reader's attention is especially drawn to Davis and Wallbridge (1981) and Phillips (1988). In fact amongst the numerous papers there are several which repeat, even if they re-work, his central themes, and some of the published collections on occasion duplicate the same papers. Nearly all of the longer single work *Human Nature* can be found interspersed among the papers. My own condensing of his lifetime's observation and analysis can perhaps best take its cue from the title of one of the volumes of his collected papers, *The Maturational Processes and the Facilitating Environment*. Winnicott's ideas can be followed through three major areas: the achievement of maturity; the task of mothering; and what can go wrong in this process.

The Achievement of Maturity

The Darwinian influence upon Winnicott is firstly seen in his concept of natural growth towards maturity. There is a healthy tendency towards positive development, which is seen as taking place in the context of a specific environment. Where there is correct provision, the natural maturational processes can function. This developmental model is an evolutionary one, partly because of the 'instinct' to survive (although Winnicott calls this a form of aggression); and partly because it depends upon a 'good-enough facilitating environment' (1971a: 139). What constitutes that environment is examined in more detail below. Throughout this section on the achievement of maturity I am assuming, with

Winnicott, the existence of a good-enough environment, providing at various stages the containment, the reflection and the stimulus necessary for a child's growth towards maturity. There is one other vital element: 'there is only one cure for immaturity and that is the *passage of time*' (1971a: 146, Winnicott's italics).

Body–Mind Unity

The inter-relationship of body (*soma*) and mind (*psyche*) is an essential one. 'The basis of psyche is soma, and in evolution soma came first' (1988b: 19). Indications of emotional maturity, like bodily growth, change with age, and just as physical maturity is complex so is emotional maturity. Yet 'how easy it is to take for granted the lodgement of the psyche in the body and to forget that this again is an achievement' (1988b: 122), which Winnicott describes as the 'dwelling of the psyche in the body' (1988b: 123). The psyche gradually comes to terms with the body, through 'quiet experiences and excited experiences' and from two directions, the personal and the environmental. The personal includes physical impulses, skin sensation, and muscular exercise, such as the delight of the naked baby in kicking. Indwelling also comes about through the environment, as when for instance after birth a mother holds or wraps her baby up tightly, trying in Winnicott's view to give her baby time to get adjusted to the new phenomenon of gravity. Even at the age of one year a normal infant is 'firmly rooted to the body only at certain times' and the psyche of an infant (like the psyche of an adult, for example in illness) can lose touch with the body, 'for instance when waking from deep sleep. Mothers know this, and they gradually wake an infant before lifting him or her' (1965a: 6), because they wish to prevent the panic that can come on waking, and finding the body in a different position, one with which the psyche has not yet caught up.

Another feature of body–mind is the significance of the skin, which 'is universally obviously important in the process of the localisation of the body exactly in and within the body' (1988b: 122). For this reason 'management of the skin in infant care is an important factor in the promotion of healthy living in the body' (1988b: 122). The skin, which Winnicott describes as a 'limiting membrane' (1988b: 68), acts as a type of container – Winnicott uses the image of the bubble – for the state of 'being', a term which Winnicott describes (at least as regards the child in the womb) as occurring when the pressure inside and the pressure outside are equal. 'Continuity of being is health.' But where there is impingement from outside, 'continuity of existence' is interrupted. Such impingements are inevitable, and as long as they are not 'too severe or too prolonged' the infant becomes accustomed to them. Nevertheless the 'nearly perfect' form of adaptation is when the individual moves from within the skin boundary (using an arm or leg, for example) to meet the environment. 'Environmental influences can start at a very early age to determine whether a person will go out for experience or withdraw from the world when seeking a reassurance that life is worth living' (1988b: 128). This concept of the skin as a membrane which makes contact with the outer world, and as a boundary for the inner world has some parallels in the work of the French psychoanalyst Anzieu and the 'psychic envelope' (1990; see also Bick, 1968).

Ego–Integration
The gradual movement towards body–mind unity is a major feature of the process of integration, another formulation which can too easily be taken for granted. This concept is the nearest Winnicott gets to a structure of personality, because he does not precisely follow Freud's tri-partite division into ego, id and super-ego. All three terms get mentioned but seldom together, although in a paper on ego integration Winnicott asserts almost in direct contrast with Freud that 'there is no id before ego' (1965b: 56).

To begin with the infant is unintegrated. There is 'not yet a conscious and an unconscious . . . What there is is an armful of anatomy and physiology, and added to this a potential for development into a human personality' (1988a: 89). Neither is there an ego, although Winnicott fudges the question of how it originates: 'Is there an ego from the start? The answer is that the start is when the ego starts' (1965b: 56). The development of the ego, at least whether it is weak or strong, 'depends on the actual mother and her ability to meet the absolute dependence of the actual infant at the beginning, at the stage before the infant has separated out the mother from the self' (1965b: 56–7). She provides 'good-enough ego-coverage' to help contain unthinkable anxieties, which he lists in two places (a little differently) as:

1. going to pieces;
2. falling for ever;
3. having no relationship to the body;
4. having no orientation; and
5. complete isolation because of there being no means of communication.

(1965b: 58; 1988a: 98–9)

The ego develops through integrating a sense of time and a sense of space; through linking the person of the baby with the body and body functions – the ego organizes sensory/motor events into personal inner reality; and through finding good objects: the breast, bottle, milk etc. (1965b: 59–60). Integration also involves 'coming together and feeling something' as opposed to being many bits, that a child is the same person who feels enjoyment and feels frustration, that he is the same child asleep and awake (1975: 150–1).

Winnicott links integration closely with holding, describing the achievement of integration as 'a unit', in which a growing sense of 'I am' includes the belief that 'I am seen or understood to exist by someone', which comes about through seeing in another's face 'the evidence I need that I have been recognised as a being' (1965b: 6). When integration is combined with 'the development of the feeling that one's person is in one's body', Winnicott calls this 'satisfactory personalization' (1975: 151).

Me/Not Me

As the baby begins to become integrated, in a body–mind unity, the sense of 'I AM' becomes stronger. The phrase is one which occurs frequently in Winnicott's writing, and is of course one which he linked to both Old and New Testaments (1986: 57), where 'I AM' denotes the name both of God, and of the divinity in Jesus in St John's Gospel. Another phrase which appears with some frequency in Winnicott is 'Me/Not Me' since the growing sense of 'I AM' also leads to the recognition of what is Not Me; or, put equally well the other way round, 'the early recognition of a Not-Me world' leads to 'the early establishment of the Me' (1965b: 216). As Winnicott observes in the same context, 'It will be understood that in practice these things develop gradually, and repeatedly come and go, and are achieved and lost.'

This is of course an achievement, but it carries much more with it. Winnicott writes: 'I suggest that this I AM moment is a raw moment; the new individual feels infinitely exposed. Only if someone has her arms round the infant at this time can the I AM moment be endured, or rather, perhaps, risked' (1965a: 148). There is now an inside and an outside. The 'limiting membrane' means that what is Not Me can be repudiated, and put outside the membrane. The Not-Me can be recognized as external, or is even externalized by projection. But the environment that is now outside can also be experienced as capable of, or actually, attacking.

Becoming Me or I AM involves putting a distance between oneself and others, and being caught up for the first time in the issue of who has the priority. In the development of the true self (as opposed to the compliant false self, which I examine further in a section below), inevitably to be oneself can lead to being 'disloyal to everything that is not oneself ... The most aggressive and therefore the most dangerous words in the languages of the world are to be found in the assertion I AM' (1986: 141). No wonder then that Winnicott links aggression with the establishment of *Me* and *Not-Me*: 'In the early stages, when the *Me* and the *Not-Me* are being established, it is the aggressive component that more surely drives the individual to a need for a *Not-Me* or an object that is felt to be external' (1975: 215). This is healthy aggression, almost a life force, which needs to find 'opposition' because only in being opposed does an individual tap into what Winnicott calls 'the important motility source', which strengthens the individual's sense of reality and of existing. He distinguishes this form of aggression and opposition from that which is a reaction to instinctual frustration (1975: 210–17). More weakly we might prefer to call it assertiveness, although such a term fits Winnicott's belief that 'only those who have reached a stage at which they can make this assertion [of I AM] are really qualified as adult members of society' (1986: 141).

Dependence to Independence
Just as Winnicott moves away from a strict Freudian tri-partite division of personality, so too he has little to say about the Freudian threefold developmental scheme of oral, anal and phallic (or genital) stages of sexuality. He suggests that it still holds good, and that it can be taken for granted, but the statement feels like an obligatory obeisance to Freud (1965b: 83). He often uses the phrase that a concept or idea can be 'taken for granted' in a way that may arguably avoid confrontation of the issue. Winnicott's own description of development is a different one, with no obvious links to the Freudian stages, nor indeed to Klein's paranoid–schizoid and depressive positions. It centres upon dependence and independence. He has less difficulty than Freud with the conflict between the needs of the individual and the needs of society, which Freud saw as responsible for the onset of neurosis. 'Maturity of the human being ... implies not only personal growth but also socialization. In health ... the adult is able to identify with society without too great a sacrifice of personal spontaneity' (1965b: 83). Against this, Winnicott's concept of the false self (see below) suggests that there is compromise.

Like that of Freud, Winnicott's scheme contains three categories (rather than stages, although they are similarly progressive): absolute dependence, relative dependence and the phrase 'towards independence' (1965b: 84). 'No stage can be missed or marred without ill-effect' (1964: 85).

Absolute dependence is the state which Winnicott describes when he uses the phrase 'there is no such thing as a baby' (1964: 88). As far as this stage is concerned the division I make in this chapter's sections between the infant's growth towards maturity and the mother's role is a false one. 'A baby cannot exist alone, but essentially is part of a relationship' (1964: 88). Primary maternal preoccupation is matched by absolute dependence. Relative dependence can be distinguished from absolute dependence because it is a state 'that the infant can know about' (1965b: 87). In this stage the main characteristics of mothering are that firstly there is 'a steady presentation of the world to the infant', and secondly there are minor failures in her adaptation to the child. As the child begins to get knowledge of her or his dependence, so too he or she knows when the mother is absent, and experiences anxiety; the child also learns about loss. They are, of course, relatively minor absences and losses from an adult's point of view, but they need to be kept within bounds from the infant's point of view.

There are more complex forms of identification in this stage than the simpler forms (such as the smile) in the earlier stage of absolute dependence. Out of this identification comes understanding of the mother's personal and separate existence 'and *eventually* the child comes to be able to believe in the parents' coming together which in fact led to his or her own conception' (1965b: 90, Winnicott's italics). Those who know the Kleinian view that the infant 'knows' about parental (oral) intercourse will notice the difference in Winnicott's timing here.

The third phase is 'towards independence', which 'is never absolute. The healthy individual does not become isolated, but becomes related to the environment in such a way that the individual and the environment can be said to be interdependent' (1965b: 84) The environment he refers to here is of course not the eco-system which is so much our concern today, although starting from mother's 'facilitating environment' he does suggest the image of concentric circles and a movement of independence outwards, to both parents and family, school – 'Latency is the period of school playing a role as a substitute for home' (1965b: 92) – and wider society. 'In ever-widening circles of social life the child is identified with society, because local society is a sample of the self's personal world as well as being a sample of truly external phenomena' (1965b: 91). The outermost circle to which a person relates might be called government: Winnicott shows his interest in this area in various papers on democracy and 'The Mother's Contribution to Society' (1986: 239–59 and 123–7 respectively).

Adaptation to Reality

In the stage of relative dependence the infant begins to come to terms with external reality. Giving up absolute dependence, and the state of being in a symbiotic relationship with mother, also means giving up omnipotence. As long as the mother has continuously adapted to her baby, her baby cannot help but believe that everything happens as he or she wants it, as if by magic. In fact Winnicott is not content with the simple phrase 'by magic', preferring to see the omnipotence of the baby as including a deep sense of having *created* what he or she wants (1965b: 180). The mother's role includes helping to create the illusion of omnipotence.

In the stage of relative dependence she acts as a buffer between the child and the outside world, introducing him or her to reality. At first this is found in herself as a representative of the world, perceived for the first time as external, and as objective instead of purely subjective. She introduces herself as separate by failing to adapt (in minor ways) as she had adapted before. Her failure to adapt enables the child to adapt to external reality – such as the reality that he or she is not omnipotent. Nevertheless Winnicott gives this a particular slant, because he sees the roots of later creativity in the baby's belief in its own creativity, and he understands illusion and disillusion as being a perpetual state that goes on throughout life. He suggests that 'the task of reality-acceptance is never completed, that no human being is free from the strain of relating inner and outer reality, that relief from this strain is provided by an intermediate area of experience which is not challenged (arts, religion, etc.)' (1975: 240).

Just as the concept of independence leads him to an interest in the dynamics of society and politics, his ideas on primitive creativity, illusion and transitional objects (see below) lead to his own theory of the meaning of art and religion. This is again different from Freud's: art for Winnicott comes from the early fantasy of, for example, creating the breast, whereas in Freud art is the sublimation of sexuality. Religion in Freud's theory is reduced to the status of an illusion, whereas for Winnicott religion, critical though he is of some aspects of it, can be expressed more positively. 'To a child who has started life in this way [being cared for reliably] the idea of goodness and of a reliable and personal parent or God can follow naturally.' But the child 'cannot be given the idea of a personal God *as a substitute for infant-care*' (1965b: 97, Winnicott's italics).

Furthermore, whereas Freud sees maturity as acceptance of the reality principle, Winnicott believes that knowledge of reality is never fully attained, and that indeed the individual person always remains, to some extent, *'an isolate, permanently non-communi-cating, permanently unknown, in fact unfound'* (1965b: 187, Winnicott's italics). The core of the self 'never communicates with the world of perceived objects'. It is culture (like mother in a person's infancy) that forms an intermediate space through which the individual and the world communicate.

The Development of Intellect

In addition to psyche and soma Winnicott is also interested in the development of mind, of thinking and of the intellect. It is the intellectual processes, quite clearly developed by the end of the first year, that enable the infant to account for and so to allow for failures in mother's adaptation. 'In this way the mind is allied to the mother and takes over part of her function' (1965a: 7). The mind serves to 'catalogue events, and to store up memories and classify them . . . to make use of time as a measurement and also to measure space. The mind also relates cause and effect' (1965a: 7). Most mothers can adapt to their child's mental capacity, although mothers can go too fast for a child limited in intellectual capacity, or they may be too slow for a quick child. In his paper 'New Light on Children's Thinking' (1989b) Winnicott suggests that where there are such failures, or where mothering is erratic, it is the mind that enables the baby to survive. Thinking can become a substitute for maternal care.

Nevertheless, such understanding in the baby can be 'too much' and lead the baby 'to develop a false self in terms of a life in the split-off mind' (1986: 59), the true self hiding in the psyche–soma. In an intellectually agile lecture to teachers, where Winnicott plays with the functions of mathematics as symbols of personality structure and mind, he says 'while higher mathematics gets a boost, the child fails to know what to do with one penny' (1986: 59). Intellectualism becomes a defence: 'a person with rich intellectual endowment in terms of grey matter can function brilliantly without much reference to the human being. But it is the human being who, by an accumulation of experiences duly assimilated, may achieve wisdom. The intellect only knows how to talk about wisdom' (1986: 60).

Guilt and the Capacity for Concern

Winnicott stresses in several places that morality is also a natural feature of human development, one which does not rely on being taught by parents, schools, churches and society (1965b: 93–105; 1986: 148–9). Guilt is not 'a thing to be inculcated' (1965b: 15). It is usually experienced as a healthy sign of development in an infant whose mother, by her 'reliable presence' (1965b: 77), provides the opportunity for the baby firstly to experience his or her instinctual wishes, and secondly to make reparation for his or her aggressive and loving feelings and desires. Winnicott hovers between aggression in the Kleinian sense of wanting ruthlessly to scoop out of the mother everything that is good in her, and his own term 'primitive love impulse' which is perhaps less pejorative and adultomorphic than the term 'aggression'. Davis and Wallbridge observe that 'this part of this theory owes much to Melanie Klein' (1981: 74), and that like her Winnicott places the origins of guilt in the first year of life: 'Ruthlessness gives way to ruth, unconcern to concern' (1965b: 23–4). This is of course just the beginning of a long process composed of innumerable repetitions spread over a period of time.

However, 'guilt is not felt, but it lies dormant, or potential, and appears (as sadness or a depressed mood) only if opportunity for reparation fails to turn up' (1965b: 77). It is significant the way Winnicott turns the relationship between guilt and reparation on its head. We might think that reparation follows the felt sense of guilt, but he suggests rather that unless there can be reparation guilt cannot be consciously felt. This appears in the latter of two papers on the subject ('The Development of the Capacity for Concern', 1965b: 73–82), where there is a more positive note: it is confidence in a benign cycle that helps modify guilt so that it approximates more to concern. The 1958 paper on guilt (1965b: 15–28) takes a slightly different position, the limited and negative Kleinian view that morality and concern are a reaction to hate. It is in the later paper that Winnicott stresses how important it is not always to interpret reparative and constructive feelings and actions of a patient as signs of an unconscious wish to destroy. It is rather by interpreting the destructive wishes that the patient can then become open to their capacity for concern. 'But constructive effort is false and meaningless unless . . . one has first reached to the destruction' (1965b: 81).

The capacity for concern is a further development upon the growing sense of guilt. Whereas the negative term guilt is linked to anxiety and ambivalent feelings, and 'implies a degree of integration in the individual ego that allows for the retention of good object-imago along with the idea of a destruction of it', concern covers the same phenomenon but 'implies further integration, and further growth, and relates in a positive way to the individual's sense of responsibility, especially in respect of relationships into which the instinctual drives have entered' (1965b: 73). It is more than reparation: it involves wanting to make a contribution to the other.

It also 'provides one of the fundamental constructive elements of play and work' (1965b: 77).

Creativity and the Ability to Play

'Play is the universal', writes Winnicott in a key phrase in one of several essays devoted to the topic in *Playing and Reality* (1971a). 'Playing facilitates growth and therefore health; playing leads into group relationships; playing can be a form of communication in psychotherapy' (1971a: 41). He implies in the same context that the analyst owes as much to 'the natural and universal thing called playing' as to Freud. Unlike many analysts before him Winnicott does not link play with erotic pleasure: indeed, if play becomes too physically exciting the play stops or is spoiled (1971a: 39). That is not to say that play is not exciting, because it is in another sense, in 'the precariousness of the interplay of personal psychic reality and the experience of control of actual objects' (1971a: 47). It may arouse anxiety, but play can still be highly satisfying even when it does. 'Anxiety is always a factor in a child's play, and often it is a major factor' (1964: 144). While play may be a way of mastering anxiety, ideas and impulses, too much anxiety, like too much excitement, can destroy playing.

Play starts in the movement of separation from mother, where 'the playground is a potential space between the mother and the baby or joining mother and baby' (1971a: 47: note his paradoxical use of two words, 'between' and 'joining'). I have referred above to the stage of relative dependence and the need for a child's fantasy to be encouraged, to create a world of her or his own, and 'to populate the world with samples of his or her own life' (1965b: 91). The next stage in the development of play is one where the child plays alone, in the presence of someone. 'Responsible persons must be available when children play; but this does not mean that the responsible person need enter into the children's playing' (1971a: 50). The last of Winnicott's stages of play is one where children allow mother to introduce both her own playing, and her own ideas for play that are not their own. 'Thus the way is paved for playing together in a relationship' (1971a: 48).

Play is a central concept in Winnicott, both in his theory of development, and in his practice as a paediatrician and therapist. It leads in two linked directions, each of which is given importance in two chapters that follow his description of play: the search for the self (1971a: 53–64), and creativity (1971a: 65–85). Play, in common with art and religious practice, is one of a number of 'allied ways towards unification and general integration of the personality' (1964: 145). It is in playing (and Winnicott boldly says 'only in playing', 1971a: 54) that the child or the adult is able to be creative and use the whole personality. He also says that no communication is possible except through playing. Later, in writing that 'in these highly specialized conditions the individual can come together and exist as a unit', it also appears that Winnicott is using the terms 'play' and 'communication' in highly specialized ways. Indeed, he asks the reader not to lose the word creativity in the sense of 'the successful or acclaimed creation', but to keep it 'to the meaning that refers to a colouring of the whole attitude to external reality' (1971a: 65). Elsewhere he describes play as 'the continuous evidence of creativity, which means aliveness' (1964: 144).

While it is of course possible to agree that creation can arise out of chaos and what he calls 'desultory formless functioning' (1971a: 64) – indeed, the creation myths of the ancient Near East contain this essential insight – Winnicott appears to narrow the possibilities of communication and creativity down to particular definitions, and to deny the creativity and communication that is possible through form and order. Sometimes indeed his own writing has that chaotic quality, where he moves from one subject to another in almost free associative style – there is one such major shift in his chapter on creativity where he shifts into a long case example and discussion of bisexuality, on the slender basis 'that creativity is one of the common denominators of men and women' (1971a: 72–85). In fact creativity is not mentioned again in that chapter. One could wish in some of his writing that when Winnicott creatively opened up new ways of experiencing, he could settle for just a little more order in his communication of his ideas! Nevertheless, Winnicott's concepts have a major contribution to make to an understanding discussion of artists and the arts (see for example Fuller, 1988). He breaks away from an anal stage explanation of creativity as 'productions', and pushes a stage further Freud's view – that art is the only form of sublimation that successfully combines the pleasure and reality principles – into a third arena of 'potential space'.

The Capacity to Be Alone

Winnicott often puts forward a particular emphasis which changes psychoanalytic ideas from negative psychopathology to positive indications of potential. He observes, for example, that psycho-analytic literature tends to write about the fear or the wish to be alone: 'a discussion of the *positive* aspects of the capacity to be alone is overdue'. 'This capacity', he writes, 'is one of the most important signs of maturity in emotional development' (1965b: 29).

This capacity is based in its origins on a paradox, the '*experience of being alone, as an infant and small child, in the presence of mother'* (1965b: 30, Winnicott's italics). He calls this ego-relatedness, a relationship where at least one of two people is alone, but where the presence of the other is important. It is this that makes his explanation a little different from those of other analytic writers, such as Klein, who says that the capacity depends on the existence of a good object in the internal world of the individual. Winnicott accepts that in time the mother who provides support is internalized, but he insists that this comes about through the experience of enjoying being alone, for a limited period, with a reliable mother, who makes no demands. The infant is then able to become unintegrated (or more accurately, to return temporarily to a state of unintegration), and to experience sensations and impulses as real and personal. Winnicott carries this further, taking perhaps as his cue a suggestion made earlier in his paper, that after satisfactory sexual intercourse each person is content to be alone. He speculates about the possibility of an 'ego orgasm': 'In the normal person a highly satisfactory experience such as may be obtained at a concert or at the theatre or in a friendship may deserve such a term' (1965b: 35). He admits that the choice of the phrase may be unwise – although he is trying at the same time to describe this type of ecstasy in climactic terms. In introducing the phrase he perhaps wants to 'pay tribute to the importance of ego-relatedness per se', although the proper comparison is not with sexual climax, but with 'the happy play of a child' (1965b: 35).

Klein too wrote a paper on loneliness (1975: 300–13), which appeared after Winnicott's. Although he acknowledges her influence, she makes no reference to him. It is instructive to compare them, since Klein stresses the integration of split-off parts, whereas Winnicott places his emphasis on a return to a state of unintegration in the presence of the mother. Both suggest that the ability to be alone comes through the response of the infant to mother's presence and affection, thus helping the internalization of a good object to take place. Klein, like Winnicott, speculates about creativity, but relates it more to the infant's gratitude and the wish to return the goodness received from mother. Winnicott, as I have indicated, places it rather in 'the individual's genetically determined tendency to be alive and to stay alive' (1986: 42). The other major difference in their papers on loneliness and being alone is in the significance that each attaches to the natural environment. Klein cites a case of a patient in whom love of nature was a sublimation of his loneliness – 'in loving nature he had actually, as he put it, "taken in an integrated object"' (1975: 307). Nevertheless, she still sees this as defensive. Nature is a substitute for the mother. Winnicott, by contrast, sees the mother as part of the total environment and cites one of Searles' least known, but profound works, on *The Nonhuman Environment* (1960). Nature, as one might expect of Winnicott as a neo-Darwinian, is not a defence: it is the 'outside world' (1964) to which the mother introduces her baby in small doses, an external world which can enrich the fundamental isolation of the inner world.

Adolescence

This important part of the developmental process has particular features, which are discussed by Winnicott in two papers (1965a: 79–87; 1971a: 138–50). Tongue in cheek he speaks of the 'one real cure for adolescence' as 'the passage of time', which together with the gradual maturational processes 'do in the end result in the emergence of the adult person' (1965a: 79). In these papers Winnicott comes closer to the traditional Oedipal position, although again his particular slant is distinct: instead of the wish to murder one parent and possess the other, Winnicott stresses the need to kill both parents off (and yet for them to survive). Similarly he gives rather more stress to the 'id' or instinctual impulses, than in his writing on infancy (not that the id is altogether forgotten there). Perhaps this is because one of the features of the onset of puberty is the force of the sexual feelings, as well as the actual physical power that the adolescent has 'to destroy and even to kill, a power which did not complicate feelings of hatred at the toddler age . . . It is like putting new wine into old bottles' (1965a: 80). The strength of the sexual feelings often leads to 'urgent masturbatory activity', which 'may be at this stage a repeated getting rid of sex, rather than a form of sex experience . . . a relief from sexual tension' (1965a: 81).

Aggression is similarly a powerful feature of this age. 'If the child is to become adult, then this move is achieved over the dead body of an adult' (1971a: 145). He means, of course, in fantasy, and often unconscious fantasy as well, although 'somewhere in the background is a life-and-death struggle'. The richness of the adolescent experience will be lost if there is not a clash between parents and their offspring, in which it may be felt; 'You sowed a baby and you reaped a bomb' (1971a: 145). There has to be real confrontation. For healthy development the adolescent needs 'to avoid the false solution . . . to feel real or to tolerate not feeling at all . . . to defy in a setting in which dependence is met and can be relied on to be met . . . to prod society repeatedly so that society's antagonism is made manifest, and can be met with antagonism' (1965a: 85).

The other feature which Winnicott stresses is the need for the adolescent to be allowed to be immature, even if the adolescent is not aware of it in himself or herself. 'Immaturity is an essential element of health at adolescence . . . in this is constrained the most exciting features of creative thought, new and fresh feeling, ideas for new living' (1971a: 146). Some of his thinking on adolescence bears resemblance to Erikson's (for example, Erikson, 1965: 254–5), although while Winnicott refers to him in other contexts he surprisingly does not do so in relation to this stage of development. Like Erikson, Winnicott appreciated the need for society 'to be shaken by the aspirations of those who are not responsible', although the last thing that adults must do to adolescents is to abdicate, because that leads the adolescent to premature and false adulthood (1971a: 146).

Winnicott only refers in passing to what specifically makes for maturity in the adult. Adolescent immaturity can clearly lead to the adult who 'is able to identify with the environment, and to take part in the establishment, maintenance and alteration of the environment, and to make this identification without serious sacrifice of personal impulse' (1965a: 102). As the ultimate he posits world citizenship as 'an immense and rare achievement in the development of the individual' although he adds immediately that this is 'scarcely compatible with personal health or with freedom from the depressed mood' (1971a: 102). For most of us 'membership of a group within the total group' is as much as our maturity allows us.

The Self
A different definition of maturity might be: 'I am here, I exist here and now, and on this basis I can enter the lives of others, and without a sense of threat to my own basis for being myself' (quoted from an unpublished paper by Davis and Wallbridge, 1981: 83). The I AM or the self is a concept which runs through Winnicott's theory of human nature and development, like the ego gradually finding form and maturity through infancy, childhood, adolescent and adult life. The ego replaces the containing and holding mother, acting as a window on the world, but the self, or at least the true self, remains hidden:

> I suggest that in health there is a core to the personality that corresponds to the true self of the split personality: I suggest that this core never communicates with the world of perceived objects, and that the individual person knows that it must never be communicated with or influenced by external reality. (1965b: 187)

This sentence, Winnicott states, is the central point of his paper, 'Communicating and Not Communicating Leading to a Study of

Certain Opposites'; and Phillips calls this 'his greatest paper' (1988: 144). It is one which we could call, despite everything else that was so innovative, his central thought, a strange if fascinating one for someone who in everything else stresses relatedness.

It is people's need to remain secret that makes psychoanalysis such a threat to so many. In finding an identity for themselves, adolescents too have to remain secret and isolated (1965b: 190). The core of the personality defends against violation. 'The question is: how to be isolated without having to be insulated'; or, stated slightly differently a few pages later, there is a distinction 'between pathological withdrawal and healthy central self-communication' (1965b: 187, 190). Similarly there is a great difference between the (true) self and the false self. The latter, which I explain further below, is like the ego in being more readily identifiable, but it is a compromise solution born of having to comply with the external environment.

Winnicott recognizes some similarities between his own thinking and the concept of the self in Jung's writings (1965b: 180); and he identifies with Erikson's phrase 'Peace comes from the inner space' (Erikson, 1958; Winnicott, 1965b: 191). Like Freud before him, Winnicott is concerned with how the growing child adapts to what Freud calls the reality principle, and what Winnicott calls the external world, or reality. For Freud it is the ego that seeks to master the demands of the id, the super-ego and the external world (Freud, 1933: 110). For Winnicott the ego contains and holds the self, enabling it to relate to outer reality and to itself. The id assumes far less significance for him, and is always linked with ego-relatedness (Phillips, 1988: 100). Vital though the initial relationship is to mother's facilitating environment, and thence to the wider world, Winnicott reserves a special place for inner space in his model of maturity: 'We have to recognise this aspect of health: the non-communicating central self, for ever immune from the reality principle, and for ever silent. Here communication is not non-verbal; it is, like the music of the spheres, absolutely personal. It belongs to being alive. And in health, it is out of this that communication naturally arises' (1965b: 192).

The Task of Mothering

When Winnicott uses the term 'mother' he usually means it to signify the person who is in the mothering role – the mother might therefore be a person other than the natural mother, and may even be father (although as I indicate later, fathers in Winnicott have a special if shadowy role). He similarly uses the term 'breast' to mean 'the whole technique of being a mother to a baby' (1988a: 26). Elsewhere he uses the phrase 'first feed' to mean an actual first feed, but also in this metaphorical sense: 'not so much a matter of a single happening as a build-up of memories of events' (1988b: 101). The inclusiveness of these terms needs to be borne in mind throughout.

There is a slight bias in him towards the natural mother, because 'it is she who can reach this special state of primary maternal preoccupation without being ill' (1975: 304). 'Being ill' here refers to the 'withdrawn state, or a dissociated state, or a fugue' which in other circumstances would be classed as a disturbance of the personality, but in the case of a mother is an indication of her complete attention to her foetus and to her baby (1975: 302). Other women may be able to adapt 'well enough' through their capacity for identification with the baby. As I examine below, fathers (being men) are assumed to be better at 'doing' than at 'being', and are therefore less able to offer what a baby needs: 'a breast that *is*, not a breast that *does*' (1971a: 82, Winnicott's italics). It is therefore WOMAN (which he himself puts in capitals) that Winnicott emphasizes. 'WOMAN is the unacknowledged mother of the first stages of the life of every man and woman' (1986: 192); and 'the general failure of recognition of absolute dependence at the start contributes to the fear of WOMAN that is the lot of both men and women' (1975: 304).

Primary Maternal Preoccupation

Such grand terms seem to indicate something special: mothering is special indeed, but not rare. Winnicott writes of 'the ordinary devoted mother' (1988a: 3–14), who learns how to be, not from books but from having herself been a baby. 'She acts naturally *naturally*' he writes in that paper. Elsewhere he describes how during pregnancy the mother develops 'a state of heightened sensitivity' which lasts for a few weeks after the birth of her child. She becomes preoccupied with her child 'to the exclusion of other interests, in a way that is normal and temporary'. This state then passes, and is often repressed, leaving little memory of it once she has 'recovered' from it. But not all women can permit this. There is in some of them a 'flight into sanity'; they cannot abandon other concerns. Repressed penis envy, for example, 'leaves but little room for primary maternal preoccupation' (1975: 302).

The Facilitating Environment

The 'ordinary devoted mother', also required to be a 'good-enough' mother, provides an environment which facilitates her baby's natural maturational processes. Whereas Melanie Klein describes the infant's experience of mother as that of the 'good breast' that provides and the bad breast that frustrates, Winnicott chooses two different terms: these represent two different functions for the baby rather than two different perceptions by the baby. He coins the phrases 'object-mother' and 'environment-mother' (1965b: 75–6). The object-mother is the mother as the object of her infant's desires, the one who can satisfy the baby's needs, as well as the object towards whom the baby will express her or his hate. The environment-mother is the mother in the role of 'the person who wards off the unpredictable and who actively provides care in handling and in general management' (1965b: 75). Holding in the literal physical sense can of course at one and the same time provide for the baby's need for erotic pleasure and contain the experience and protect the baby from impingements that might mar the pleasure. She protects the baby also from those parts of herself that might intrude (for instance, her murderous feelings when her baby yells and yells, 1964: 87). She provides boundaries before time and space can be separated out. She (indeed both parents) hold boundaries when the child becomes adolescent and forcefully needs to test them out. This firm holding also enables a child (and adolescent) 'to discover impulse, and only impulse that is found and assimilated is available for self-control and socialization' (1984: 157).

The early holding and containing therefore shifts gradually into the continued provision of ego-support, which the child, the adolescent and the adult will need whenever there is excessive threat or stress. Davis and Wallbridge quote from an unpublished paper: 'A child is playing in the garden. An aeroplane flies low overhead . . . you hold the child close to yourself, and the child uses the fact that you are not scared beyond recovery, and is soon off and away, playing again' (1981: 99). The provision of such an environment can also occur in psychotherapy: the therapist provides the environment in which the patient is able to develop and mature. Winnicott also sees this environment as one in which the patient who needs to can also regress. At first glance this facilitating environment in therapy may appear close to the core conditions of person-centred therapy and counselling, but, as I shall clarify, the provision of such an environment involves much greater complexities of response and adaptation than is apparent in the basic core conditions which Carl Rogers suggests are sufficient for therapists to provide.

Adapting and Failing to Adapt

In the beginning a mother constantly adapts to her baby's needs. 'The infant at the start needs a degree of active adaptation to needs which cannot be provided unless a devoted person is doing everything' (1965a: 23). This, at this stage, is far from what later can be called 'spoiling' the child. In doing this the mother needs to be what Winnicott called 'good-enough', by which he means repeatedly meeting the omnipotence of the infant: her constant adaptation at this stage to the baby's needs provides the child with an experience of omnipotence. 'On this basis the infant can gradually abrogate omnipotence' (1965b: 146).

If an infant is to move from absolute dependence to relative dependence, a mother has to begin to fail to adapt to her baby's needs: 'in time the baby begins to need the other to fail to adapt – this failure being also a graduated process that cannot be learned from books' (1988a: 8). Of course in another sense this is still adaptation; adaptation to the need to fail to adapt. This type of failure (which as we shall see is also true of therapy itself) is essential: 'a mother who cannot gradually fail on this matter of sensitive adaptation is failing in another sense; she is failing (because of her own immaturity or her own anxieties) to give her infant reasons for anger' (1965b: 87).

The phrase 'good-enough' has become something of a by-word. It is frequently used as a consolation for not being perfect – not unnaturally given the huge demands which appear to be placed on mothers by the studies of psychologists and psychoanalysts. Nevertheless in Winnicott's writing the phrase is never used in that sense. What he constantly does stress is that mothers normally know better than doctors, paediatricians and midwives. The demands which professionals (and their books) make upon them, in terms of the way they should be with and act towards their babies, are more likely to get in the way of natural responsive mothering than to assist it. For example: 'There are very subtle things that the mother knows intuitively and without any intellectual appreciation of what is happening, and which she can only arrive at by being left alone and given full responsibility. . .' (1988a: 64). In that sense he is clearly on the side of mothers. But it would be foolish to believe that the phrase 'good-enough' means settling for mediocrity. Winnicott is quite clear that there can equally be a 'not good-enough' mother, 'who repeatedly fails to meet the infant gesture', and is unable to meet her infant's needs. This leads to compliance on the part of the baby towards her, rather than the reverse, and to the earliest stage of the false self (1965b: 145).

The Mirror

In one short but stimulating chapter on 'The Mirror-role of Mother and Family in Child Development' (1971a: 111–18), Winnicott draws upon Lacan's identification of the child's use of the mirror as a significant point in ego development (Lacan, 1949), although he makes a vital and quite distinct addition, that the mother's face, particularly in the early weeks of the infant's life, functions as a mirror of the self. Winnicott's observation has been confirmed by simultaneous video studies of the faces of parents (including fathers) and their infants in which parent and child can be clearly seen to respond to each other: it is not simply that the baby responds to the mother's smile, but that the mother also mirrors her baby's expressions. As Winnicott puts it: 'the mother is looking at the baby and what she looks like is related to what she sees there' (1971a: 112). He suggests a sequence of perception that runs:

> When I look I am seen, so I exist.
> I can now afford to look and see.
> I now look creatively and what I apperceive I also perceive.
> In fact I take care not to see what is not there to be seen (unless I am tired).
>
> (1971a: 114)

Again this responsibility on the part of the mother is 'naturally done well' although 'many babies' do not have such mothers. 'They look and they do not see themselves.' Some of them may 'look around for other ways of getting something of themselves back from the environment' (1971a: 112). The chapter contains a number of short examples from his clinical work including the poignant question of one of his patients: 'Wouldn't it be awful if the child looked into the mirror and saw nothing!' (1971a: 116; popular legend suggests that this is indeed so for vampires, whose need to suck blood appears to indicate a primitive emptiness). The brevity of the paper is tantalizing, but suggests directions in which these ideas could be taken further – the narcissism of the adolescent, the face in art, and the reflective surfaces of the environment. It is also evident that although Winnicott twice cites Lacan, his thinking (as Rudnytsky expounds at length, 1991: 70–95) is totally different: Lacan's mirror permits no place for the mother, and what the infant discovers is the self as other, rather than a unitive experience of the reflection of the self in the other.

Illusion and Disillusion

Such seeing in the mirror-face of the mother relates to actual sight (Winnicott is less sure what happens in babies born blind). Yet there is another type of seeing which involves internal images: the concept of illusion is a vital one in Winnicott's theory. He differs considerably from Freud, who in his book *The Future of an Illusion* (1927) links illusion with error. Objective and reality thinking are Freud's constant goals. He has no real sense of the *value* of illusion, except as a pathological feature which may serve a neurotic need, but has to be abandoned in the process of reality-testing. Winnicott on the other hand suggests that illusion is a constant and valuable feature into and including adult life, and that, as already quoted above, 'the task of reality-acceptance is never completed, that no human being is free from the strain of relating inner and outer reality, and that relief from this strain is provided by an intermediate area of experience which is not challenged (arts, religion, etc.)' (1975: 240; see also Chapter 4).

It is the mother who first 'affords the infant the opportunity for the *illusion* that her breast is part of the infant' (1975: 238, Winnicott's italics). She also enables the illusion that the infant has created the breast, which was offered to the baby just at the right moment, when there was 'an expectancy, a state of affairs in which the infant is prepared to find something somewhere, not knowing what' (1988b: 100). We may 'as sophisticated philosophers' know that the baby created nothing and that the breast was already there, 'but the mother by her extremely delicate adaptation to the (emotional) needs of the infant is able to allow the baby this illusion' (1988b: 101).

After the 'theoretical first feed' the baby has a definite image with which to imagine (or 'hallucinate') the breast, and from which to build up memories that in turn lead to 'confidence that the object of desire can be found, and this means that the infant gradually tolerates the absence of the object' (1988b: 106). The mother is now ready to enable disillusion to take place, so that more of the reality of the external world can be accepted (again in small doses). Disillusionment is a major task, which is only second in importance to providing the opportunity for illusion. It is necessary so that weaning can take place satisfactorily; and indeed without disillusionment it can be said that 'the mere termination of breast-feeding is not a weaning' (1975: 240). The mother promotes disillusion, as I have indicated above, by 'adapting less and less completely, gradually, according to the infant's growing ability to deal with her failure' (1975: 238).

Winnicott is certain (as is clear from the quotations above about the task of reality-acceptance) that the movement in and out of illusion and disillusion goes on throughout life. Transitional objects feature in the next stage of development, through and after weaning, and constitute a different type of illusion. But more importantly – and here we see Winnicott the philosopher more than

Winnicott the paediatrician or psychoanalyst – we can never make direct contact with external reality. There is always 'only an illusion of contact, a midway phenomenon that works very well for me when I am not tired' (1988b: 114–15). In the end all we can know is 'the essential aloneness of the human being' (1988b: 114), although Winnicott does not go so far as to consider whether this too might not be an illusion! Perhaps tongue in cheek he expostulates, 'I couldn't care less that there is a philosophical problem involved' (1988b: 115).

Transitional Objects

It may be thought that transitional objects belong to the earlier section on developmental processes, although if I am to be true to Winnicott's definition of them, they should really have a section completely to themselves, since they belong neither to the child nor to the mother, but to an area between. We should never ask the infant the question, Winnicott emphasizes through italics, *'Did you conceive of this or was it presented to you from without?'* (1975: 239–40) because the transitional object belongs to the realm of intermediate experience. It is similarly a mistake to think that a mother can provide a child with a transitional object: she can only provide a comforter, which is a substitute for herself, but is actually less important than mother. The transitional object is one which the child discovers, or even creates, and is more important than mother, 'almost an inseparable part of the infant' (1975: 235). This is seen when children hold their transitional object to their mouth or nose even when they are cuddling right up to mother. These developments take place some time between the ages of four and twelve months.

A transitional object is not strictly a teddy bear or cuddly toy. Winnicott makes it clear that it comes between the thumb (which is literally an inseparable part of the baby) and the external object such as the doll or teddy bear (1975: 229). He refers in one place to a patient's toy rabbit which is much more a comforter than a transitional object (1975: 234–5). So the transitional object is more likely to be a piece of a blanket or piece of napkin, even the wool pulled off a blanket; something that is readily available, and in one sense is provided by the mother, but never deliberately given to the child with that purpose. However, in the same paper Winnicott appears to allow a different patient's purple rabbit to be defined as transitional, and confusingly, in a paper a year later, he suggests that transitional objects include 'the thumb, or that bit of blanket, or that soft rag doll' (1975: 223). It is similarly confusing that the mother can herself be the transitional object (1975: 232). In addition Winnicott refers to transitional phenomena, such as 'mouthing, accompanied by sounds of "mum-mum", babbling, anal noises, the first musical notes, and so on' (1975: 232). These distinctions are examined more critically in Chapter 4.

The transitional object has special qualities (1975: 233, 236–7): the infant assumes rights over it, and the parents permit this. In places Winnicott calls it a possession rather than an object (his terminology again gets rather muddled over this). It is cuddled as well as loved and mutilated, and it must survive this (which makes it quite a problem for parents, since they cannot change it. Only the infant can do that!). The object has some warmth and vitality of its own, and it comes neither from without nor within. The fate of the object is that over a period of time it is 'not so much forgotten as relegated to limbo'. It is never under magical control, nor like an external object is it internalized, becoming an internal object in the Kleinian sense.

The twin concepts of illusion (above) and transitional objects naturally link, in Winnicott's writing, with a third concept, sometimes called 'intermediate state' (1975: 230), or in a later essay, 'potential space' (1971a: 107–10). Although he puts forward the idea for discussion, the area itself as he describes it is not one that can be challenged, since we do not know whether it is created by us or whether it is 'a bit of perceived reality'. It is a state of what in other circumstances might be called 'madness' (as primary maternal preoccupation in other circumstances might be called an illness). It is a state (often of play), which parents can allow children, through trust, reliability and relaxation. It is also a state which in society we can allow each other, particularly in the arts, religion, imaginative living and creative scientific work (1975: 242), as long as the person in this potential space or intermediate state does not seek to force others into sharing an 'illusion that is not their own' (1975: 231).

Allowing Immaturity
Since development is a natural process, it cannot be hurried, although it can be hindered by unresponsive or neglectful parenting. Nor can development be taught: Winnicott makes it clear time and again that a mother may encourage her baby, but she should not take over her baby's natural creative growth. Just as the transitional object cannot be given to a child, so values should not be forced upon a child. What he writes of religion is also true of other forms of knowledge: 'The good alternative [to teaching by force] has to do with the provision of those conditions for the infant and child that enable such things as trust and "belief in", and ideas of right and wrong, to develop out of the working of the individual child's inner

processes' (1965b: 94). In the same paper he writes: 'The parents do not have to make their baby as the artist has to make his picture or the potter his pot' (1965b: 96). Although he specifically refers here to a pre-verbal stage, Winnicott extends the idea of the need for the 'provision of opportunity' (1965b: 103) to subsequent developments, including communication of all kinds of cultural values. In this paper (on 'Morals and Education') he frequently suggests that parents need to 'leave lying around' not just toys that the child will pick up and play with as he or she wishes, but moral codes and other cultural phenomena (1965b: 99). He is sceptical of some parents' attempts to educate their children: 'Give a child Mozart and Haydn and Scarlatti from the beginning and you may get precocious good taste, something that can be shown off at parties. But the child probably has to start with noises blown through toilet paper over a comb . . . an appreciation of the sublime should be a personal achievement, not an implant' (1965b: 100–2).

Surviving

This point about providing opportunities and allowing for immaturity is just as strongly made when Winnicott addresses those who have adolescent children. I have noted above the need to permit adolescents to be immature. Parents need to do this from their own position of strength: 'Mature adults . . . must believe in their own maturity as never before or after' (1971a: 145). Again it is the adolescents who have to discover their own maturation, which includes their need to challenge and metaphorically to kill off their parents. Parents cannot make this happen. They 'can help only a little: the best they can do is to *survive*, to survive intact, and without changing colour, without relinquishment of any important principle' (1971a: 145, Winnicott's italics). Surviving, or staying alive, is a necessity for the parent, which Winnicott believes to be essential in the therapist as well: 'In doing psycho-analysis I aim at: keeping alive, keeping well, keeping awake' (1965b: 166).

He provides a poignant example of what happens when a parent does not survive. A child had survived a car crash in which her father had been killed. This was 'at a time when the little girl was going through a phase in which she was hating her father as well as loving him' and had pleaded with him not to go out in the car. At the scene of the accident she kicked his dead body to wake him up, but also to show her anger with him. It was only when Winnicott was able to use her kicking the wall in his consulting room that he could put this into words for her, and 'she gradually came back into life' (1965b: 21).

This chapter has already drawn heavily upon the richness of

Winnicott's own words on developmental processes and the provision of the right environment in which these can take place. There is one passage which perhaps sums up his view of the role and the experience of parents, and which needs to be reproduced in its entirety:

> If you do all you can to promote personal growth in your offspring, you will need to be able to deal with startling results. If your children find themselves at all they will not be contented to find anything but the whole of themselves, and that will include the aggression and destructive elements in themselves as well as the elements that can be labelled loving. There will be this long tussle which you will need to survive.
>
> With some of your children you will be lucky if your ministrations quickly enable them to use symbols, to play, to dream, to be creative in satisfying ways, but even so the road to this point may be rocky. And in any case you will make mistakes and these mistakes will be seen and felt to be disastrous, and your children will try to make you feel responsible for setbacks even when you are not in fact responsible. Your children simply say: I never asked to be born.
>
> Your rewards come in the richness that may gradually appear in the personal potential of this or that boy or girl. And if you succeed you must be prepared to be jealous of your children who are getting better opportunities for personal development than you had yourselves. You will feel rewarded if one day your daughter asks you to do some baby-sitting for her, indicating thereby that she thinks you may be able to do this satisfactorily; or if your son wants to be like you in some way, or falls in love with a girl you would have liked yourself, had you been younger. Rewards come *indirectly*. And of course you know you will not be thanked. (1971a: 143, Winnicott's italics)

Father and the Family

Despite his intention of 'addressing mothers and fathers directly' in *The Child, the Family and the Outside World* (1964), Winnicott plainly writes for mothers. Fathers are hardly mentioned, even where they might reasonably expect to be included. There is only one brief reference to the role of the father in the first part: 'He can help provide a space . . . Properly protected by her man, the mother is saved from having to turn outwards to deal with her surroundings at the time when she is wanting to turn inwards' (1964: 25). Father provides a secure environment for mother to provide a facilitating environment for her baby. The second part of the book starts with a chapter aptly titled 'What about father?', which indeed by this point fathers might be asking! It contains little other than a standard view of father as someone who should be encouraged to be interested in the baby, but probably has little interest or ability in these matters.

There is little sense of a specific role for father in direct relation to the child. He provides 'social security' for the mother and, through his relationship with the mother, also for the child. The parents' sexual union provides 'a hard fact around which the child can build a fantasy ... part of the natural foundation for a personal solution to the problem of the triangular relationship' (1964: 114–15). Winnicott extends this idea by referring to the special relationship a daughter may have with her father, and the problems of jealousy and rivalry between the two parents and the child, whether girl or boy. This is all standard Freudian Oedipal theory (and rather unexciting compared to much else of Winnicott's writing). It is almost a nod in the direction of what is already 'well-known' (1964: 117–18).

Father also provides 'moral support' by backing mother's authority, and standing for law and order: 'He does not have to be there all the time to do this, but he has to turn up often enough for the child to feel that he is real and alive' (1964: 115). Finally, father provides a model both of men and also of the world of work to which he goes off each morning and returns each night. If this emasculated view of fatherhood were not enough, a remark in the penultimate paragraph of this chapter makes the final cut, where Winnicott suggests 'that it is mother's responsibility to send father and daughter, or father and son, out together for an expedition every now and again' (1964: 118).

The criticisms of Winnicott's theory and practice are reserved for Chapter 4, where the weakness of his theory about fathers is one area of concern. He was a man of his time, and perhaps even today there are more homes than the 'new man' of liberal middle-class thinking recognizes, where Winnicott's picture of the distant, half-engaged father would be found. The weakness is that there is no sense of an alternative, such as feminist psychotherapists suggest, except for occasional passing references to 'the maternal aspect of the father' (1988a: 93n), which are no more than a nod in the direction of challenging gender roles.

Similarly, despite its title, *The Child, the Family and the Outside World* has little to say about the family. For this we need to look elsewhere (1965a: 40–9, 88–94; 1986: 128–41). There the family's role is if anything given rather more importance than father's, although there is more value given to the relationship with father in helping the child to view mother differently, from father's perspective. Father helps separation to take place. Winnicott calls this a 'to-and-fro experience' where the child moves from one parent to another, or even more widely through the extended family, to 'an aunt or a grandmother or a big sister' (1986: 138, where we note the absence of any other men in this extended family!). Essentially the family provides a rather wider environment, similar to that which mother originally provides, in which play, feelings of love and hate, sympathy and tolerance, as well as exasperation, rivalry and disloyalty can be tested out. 'When a family is intact and is a going concern over a period of time each child derives benefit from being able to see himself or herself in the attitude of the individual members or in the attitudes of the family as a whole . . . This could be one way of stating the contribution that a family can make to the personality growth and enrichment of each one of its individual members' (1971a: 118). Although the family provides this for the child, the relationship is reciprocal, the child also providing new situations for the family: 'children produce a family around them, perhaps by needing something, something which we give because of what we know about expectation and about fulfilment. We see what the children create when playing at families, and we feel that we want to make real the symbols of their creativeness' (1971a: 47). In turn 'the family leads on to all manner of groupings, groupings that get wider and wider until they reach the size of the local society and society in general' (1986: 140).

Winnicott is certainly not at his best when writing about relationships beyond the mother–infant couple. He admits himself that so much has been written about the family that it is difficult to say anything original (1986: 128), although he actually has more interesting ideas about the family than he does about the father–child relationship. His true originality lies elsewhere, and it is that upon which it is more useful to concentrate.

A Classification for Disorders

This chapter has concentrated upon the normal processes of development. Winnicott devotes considerable space to this and probably wrote more about normality than psychopathology. He puts forward what essentially is a positive developmental model based upon natural processes and a good-enough beginning, through which continuity is preserved, and the individual 'really starts and eventually comes to feel real, and to experience life appropriate to his or her emotional age' (1965b: 138). Normal development, even when it runs relatively smoothly, inevitably involves the development of different defences, and personal characteristics which will influence inter-personal relationships 'with whole people', and may lead to what are classified as psycho-neurotic symptoms. When Winnicott writes that 'we are poor indeed if we are only sane' (1965a: 61) he perhaps refers primarily to the ability to stay in touch with more psychotic parts of ourselves, but the axiom applies as much to neurotic variations upon normality.

Winnicott is really not very interested in his written work on these more neurotic problems, except in relation to the cultivation of a false self, which is sometimes mistaken (even by analysts) for the real self. The therapist has to be careful not to treat symptoms presented in the false self, since '*only the true self can be analysed*' (1965b: 133, Winnicott's italics). The false self is a natural part of development, 'built up on a basis of compliance . . . a defensive function, which is the protection of the true self' (1965b: 133). This is of course a necessary defence, leading to a 'social manner' and a 'compromise', although in health it is a way of being that ceases to be maintained when the issues are vital ones: at this point 'the True Self is able to override the compliant self' (1965b: 150). However, there are degrees of the false self, so that it can become 'a kind of sublimation, as when a child grows up to be an actor'; or a split can develop between the false self and the true self, hiding the true self and leading to 'poor capacity for using symbols, and a poverty of cultural living' (1965b: 150); or intellectual activity becomes the seat for the false self, which can lead to dissociation from psychosomatic being (1965b: 144); or 'when the false self becomes exploited and treated as real there is a growing sense in the individual of futility and despair' (1965b: 133).

The 'false self' (like the true self it is sometimes capitalized, sometimes not), Winnicott suggests, is 'a valuable classificatory label . . . not uncommon . . . The defence is massive and may carry with it considerable social success. The indication for analysis is that the patient asks for help because of feeling unreal or futile in spite of the apparent success of the defence' (1965b: 134).

Another classification, in which Winnicott shows considerable interest, especially in his pioneering work with regressed patients, is psychotic illness. The origins of this he places firmly in environmental failure, rather than in constitutional or hereditary factors. Psychosis (or schizophrenia) may be masked by the development of the false self; may be latent in the 'brittleness' of success in children who pass for normal (1965b: 59); or may be hidden in the schizoid personality. Where there is a breakdown, it is a return to a breakdown that has already been; or where there is fear of breakdown, it is fear of a breakdown that has already happened. Breakdown means the failure of defences which were organized around the original breakdown at the stage of dependence on maternal ego-support (1965b: 139). Lack of ego-support may come about through 'maternal disorders', such as the inability of a woman to be preoccupied with her baby, or through a mother who is pathologically preoccupied with her baby, through 'lending her own self to the infant' (1965a: 16). In the latter case the illusion of omnipotence is not given up, and the baby enters into a state of delusion.

Environmental failure to facilitate the maturational processes is linked to 'mental illness of the mental hospital type, psychosis'. This type of failure Winnicott calls 'privation' (1965b: 226), and is to be distinguished from 'deprivation', which he uses to describe 'failure on top of success', that is, 'there was good-enough environment, and then this stopped' (1965b: 226), at a point when the child was able to perceive actual deprivation. He or she knew that the cause of depression or disintegration was external, and not internal, which makes all the difference, since the child then seeks 'a cure by new environmental provision' (1975: 313). The particular form of behaviour which Winnicott associates with deprivation (although it surely cannot be the only one, as his concentration upon it suggests?) is the antisocial tendency. This he underlines *is not a diagnosis* (1975: 308). It is rather a sign of a period of hope, in which the child (or adult) draws attention to the need for someone to attend to the management of their environment. The antisocial tendency (he gives two main examples, stealing and destructiveness) can be found in the normal individual, or in someone who is neurotic or psychotic, although confusingly, in another context, he classifies the antisocial tendency as 'between these two [neurosis and psychosis]' (1965b: 138). Unlike these other categories of psycho-neurosis and psychosis, the antisocial tendency is to be treated not by psychoanalysis (or psychotherapy), but by 'the provision of child care which can be rediscovered by the child, and into which the child can experiment again with the id impulses' (1975: 315).

Elsewhere Winnicott explores other features of psychopathology, such as regression, the manic defence, dissociation, disintegration, character disorders and aggression as well as specific symptoms such as fidgetiness and feeding problems (see various papers in 1965b and 1975). Some aspects of his approach to these and other clinical situations are described further in Chapter 3.

Summary

Throughout Winnicott's theories of maturational processes and the facilitating environment it is not difficult to find parallels between the growth of the child and the course of effective therapy, and between the role of the parent and the role of the therapist. Like mother, the therapist provides space, with secure boundaries, in which trust in the relationship can be experienced. Primary maternal preoccupation might be the therapist's intention during the therapy hour (even if some patients do not permit it). Sensitive adaptation to what a patient can take and allow, or wants, is similarly an essential part of the process. Like a mother, the therapist gradually allows the inner and external worlds of the patient to impinge and be experienced 'in small doses', protecting from too much where necessary, and encouraging access when required. Development can only take place at the pace of the patient and, again like a mother, the therapist is careful in what he or she gives; it is much better that patients discover for themselves. An interpretation should come from the patient, who needs to feel that he or she has created it. As Winnicott writes of one situation: 'It was not my job to give this link to my patient in this session because the patient is essentially discovering things for herself, and premature interpretation in such circumstances annihilates the creativity of the patient and is traumatic in the sense of being against the maturational process' (1971a: 117).

He never under-estimates the difficulties involved, but there is always a message of hope, not only in a patient being ill at all (he sees both regression and the antisocial tendency as such signs of hope), but also in the corrective experience of therapy. Good technique *may* provide this: 'in analysis a patient may for the first time get full attention from another person . . . or may for the first time be in contact with someone who is capable of being objective' (1965b: 258). Nevertheless, a corrective experience is never enough, and it is the failures, 'often quite small ones', that enable the patient to hate the therapist, and to bring the original environmental failures into the transference. The survival of the therapist, as I have already indicated, is as important in therapy as the survival of the parent in child and adolescent development. Even if 'in the end we succeed by failing' (1965b: 258), this is again similar to what Winnicott says is inevitable in parenting. It does in fact provide a rather different example of a corrective experience, because this time, for some reason we can never be sure of, our failure succeeds in helping the patient develop.

Whether therapy has anything in it that is similar to the transitional object is open to question, although in some sense it may be a transitional phenomenon in itself. Whether it quite qualifies to be 'potential space' *per se* is doubtful, although its provision of the opportunity for potential space is likely. It provides space to play, to create illusions and to move through disillusion-ment into new perceptions of and approximations to reality; although at the same time therapy is certainly not all play: when highly charged emotions are felt and expressed play is certainly not possible, and the image of play (in its pure sense) may be a more poetic fancy than the often ruthless or even prosaic reality of therapy suggests. Therapy hopefully leads to some breaking free from the false self, and to the development of a less compliant and more integrated personal core. Winnicott himself is under no illusion that this task of 'good enough adaptation' in order to enable 'a shift in the patient of the main site of operation from a false to a true self' is anything less than 'exacting'. 'The analyst is not, after all, the patient's natural mother' (1975: 298–9).

Despite this major difference, there are obvious parallels between the role of the mother and the role of the therapist in facilitating maturity. Some of these will become clearer as I move in the next chapter into a closer examination, from his own and others' experiences, of Winnicott as a psychotherapist and paediatrician in practice.

3

Major Contributions to Practice

Paediatrician and Psychoanalyst

Winnicott's papers demonstrate that his contributions to the development of theory come from an extensive and deeply rooted clinical experience. The dedication of *Playing and Reality* (1971a) is 'To my patients who paid to teach me'. In the introduction to the same book Winnicott writes that 'direct clinical observations of babies . . . have indeed been the basis for everything I have built up into theory' (1971a: xiii). Similarly, in the preface to his *Collected Papers: Through Paediatrics to Psycho-Analysis*, he describes his contributions as 'testing out my own ideas as they came to me in the course of my clinical work' (1975: ix). There are a large number of papers, but only just over half were published in book form during his lifetime, which is perhaps an indication of where his priorities lay: Winnicott devoted himself to his patients, to his students and colleagues, and to addressing meetings involving all kinds of professions, rather than making much of his written work ready for what would have been certain publication.

His writing comes alive partly because of the immediacy of his style, but also because he is liberal with examples from his consultations. Many who write about Winnicott point to the sheer volume of his experience, particularly with children. He himself refers to personally taking 20,000 case histories in his first 25 years as a physician and psychiatrist in a hospital setting (1965a: 160n). The editor of *The Piggle* refers to an estimate of 60,000 mothers and children seen over a period of forty years (1980: xii). Winnicott added that he saw 'some hundreds' for individual psychotherapy (1965b: 115). This is a vast accumulation of material to draw upon.

But the particular source of his observations needs to be borne in mind. Much of the time Winnicott writes about mothers and babies, children and adolescents. He also writes powerfully about the regressed patient, with clearly many of the same phenomena on view in those adults who live through the traumatic (*and* positive) experiences of infancy and childhood. We have to ask how much of his practice is specific to the context in which he worked. We must not make the assumption (without testing it out) that what he writes is necessarily applicable to that major part of therapy that is classically defined as working with 'neurotic' rather than 'psychotic' elements in the client. One of the key questions we need to ask is this: are some aspects of Winnicott's technique only applicable to some of the deeply disturbing situations he had to deal with? Or does he also set out new markers for counselling and therapy generally? It is wise to bear in mind that in these more extreme situations even Winnicott was only prepared to work with one such patient at a time. Little tells us how 'he spoke of patients having to "queue up" sometimes to go into such a state [full regression], one waiting until another had worked through it and no longer needed him in that way' (1990: 47–8). But despite this particular caution to those tempted to emulate him, it is also clear, as is shown in many examples in this chapter, that in his therapeutic interactions generally Winnicott could be spontaneous, open and even outspoken in a way with which we are not normally familiar in the context of psychoanalysis.

In building up this picture of Winnicott in his practice, we are fortunate in having first-hand evidence from some of his colleagues as well as some of his patients. We also have Winnicott's own short examples in his papers, and occasional more extensive descriptions. Margaret Little has written movingly about her analysis with him, over a continuous period of six years, providing perhaps the most complete picture we shall ever have of Winnicott's style in the face of psychotic material (Little, 1985 and 1990, the latter being a slightly fuller reprint of the former). We are fortunate too in having Guntrip's account of a second analysis with Winnicott, following his first with Fairbairn (Guntrip, 1975). Winnicott himself wrote up various case-notes for publication, including his first book, *Clinical Notes on Disorders of Childhood* (1931) and one of the last he himself prepared, *Therapeutic Consultations in Child Psychiatry* (1971b). Both books concern his work with children and adolescents, as does the posthumously published account of the psychoanalytic treatment of a little girl, *The Piggle* (1980). The fullest account by Winnicott himself of analysis with an adult patient first appeared in a short paper called 'Withdrawal and Regression' (Winnicott, 1975) but has been added to extensively from his case-notes in another posthumous work, *Holding and Interpretation: Fragment of an Analysis* (1989a).

It is on these accounts that I chiefly draw, firstly looking at key aspects of his work as a paediatrician and child analyst; secondly, looking at his adaptive style with deeply regressed patients, including the importance of recognizing hate in the counter-transference; and thirdly isolating some features from his therapy with less disturbed adult patients. There are some glimpses of him as a supervisor and teacher to which I briefly refer. While it is important not to neglect Winnicott's other area of expertise, with children and adolescents in special settings, such as evacuees in the Second World War, or in residential care (Winnicott, 1984), space only permits one or two examples from these situations. In Chapter 5 I develop further this side of his expertise, when I look at his influence upon other caring professions.

Working with Children

Masud Khan describes first meeting Winnicott in 1949 at the Paddington Green Clinic:

> he was amidst five children. All drawing, or what he would call doodling, with him, plus their parents. Winnicott would move from child to child, then go to the parents of the particular child, talk with them and come back, and so on. I witnessed this for two hours. (Clancier and Kalmanovitch, 1987: xvi–xvii)

Professor John Davis recalls the time when as a junior doctor himself he first got to know the consultant paediatrician Winnicott in his outpatient clinic at Paddington Green Hospital – this was before the days of the National Health Service. It was 'quite unlike any other that I had sat in on, though later, in the so-called Third World, I came across colleagues who worked in much the same way' (Davis, 1993). (Winnicott's own description of the setting in a paper in 1941, referred to below, differs from these eye-witness accounts, although his practice may have changed since it is a few years before Davis or Khan first met him.) Davis paints a vivid picture of a large waiting area milling with families, amongst whom Winnicott moved, seeing his patients in that context, not in a separate room as is now usually the case in any hospital. He could of course take note of other families at the same time, while dealing principally with particular patients.

'He took a careful history, made a thorough physical examination (he enjoyed handling his patients and regarded it as therapeutic as well as diagnostic) and kept good notes' (Davis, 1993). This parenthesis is significant: Winnicott appears in some ways to have been much more like a mother than a father figure in this context (and perhaps in others too, attracting what is known as a maternal transference). His pleasure in touching his child patients should not of course be either regarded as solely a feminine trait, or treated with suspicion by a later age that has gone too far in pathologizing a man's pleasure in children. Nevertheless there was that about Winnicott that was as comfortable with the 'feminine' as with the 'masculine' in him (such terms are not ideal, and are in any case open to question: indeed his almost sole writing on gender (1971a: 72–84) supports my suggestion that feminine and masculine both find their expression in him). As one correspondent told me, if you heard him on the phone you could not be sure from the pitch of his voice whether you were talking to a woman or a man. I include this minor detail (and recall too, as referred to in Chapter 1, the question of impotence that appears to have arisen in his own analysis), not in any attempt to psychoanalyse him, but to draw attention to what may have been a very finely developed sense in him (partly reflected physically?), that in turn might help us recognize just how much he was able to enter into the experience of mothers and babies.

In his obituary and eulogy at Winnicott's funeral (referred to briefly in Chapter 1) Sir Peter Tizard said that he had the most astonishing powers with children. He recounted a story about Winnicott who was due to visit a Danish family for a second time after an interval of some years. The children were delighted that they would meet him again, remembering how he had played with them, and how he had spoken their language. Their father found it difficult to convince them that their memory was false, since Winnicott could not speak a word of Danish (Tizard, 1971).

It is not surprising, given his gift for such work, that Winnicott felt some concern about calling his work with children 'a technique'. 'No two cases are alike, and there is much more free interchange between the therapist and the patient than there is in a straight psycho-analytic treatment' (1971b: 1). He was certain that he could apply psychoanalysis to child psychiatry, and that it was the basis of his work, although in his introduction to *Therapeutic Consultations in Child Psychiatry* (1971b) he writes that he does not believe the work itself is psychoanalysis. On the other hand, he writes elsewhere of treating children through psychoanalysis (of which the little girl in *The Piggle* is one example). He states that 'the borders [between psychiatry, psychotherapy and psychoanalysis] are so vague that I would be unable to be exact' (1965b: 115). He was more interested in what he did with the transference and the unconscious than in the formal arrangements of the session.

If Winnicott did not like the idea of a technique, he nonetheless developed particular methods in working with children, promoting through play the relationship between himself and the child (including special types of play such as the spatula game and the squiggle). The play also provided possibilities for understanding a child more deeply. Play was the main method of communication. He wanted the child first of all to enjoy the experience, but also partly 'to get meaning out of a game' (1980: 175). He summarizes the many different dimensions of the theory of play as 'exciting and precarious' (1971a: 51–2).

The Spatula Game

Winnicott's gift for detailed observation is one I have already noted. Nowhere is this more clearly evidenced than in his paper 'The Observation of Infants in a Set Situation' (1975: 52–69; references in this section are to this paper unless otherwise stated; see also his later paper on a similar theme in 1965b, 109–14).

The 'set situation' is Winnicott's clinic, a 'fairly large room' which he chose because 'so much can be seen and done in the time that it takes the mother and her child to reach me from the door at the opposite end of the room'. The interval and the space also gave Winnicott time to make facial contact with mother and child. The child in this instance is between five and thirteen months, after which time this particular game ceases to have the same interest.

As a matter of routine Winnicott placed a shiny metal spatula at the edge of the table, close enough for the child to reach. Mothers often intuitively knew what this was about, although he would also explain that for a period of time he and she 'should contribute as little as possible to the situation, so that what happens can fairly be put down to the child's account'. He did not wish to influence the child by facial expression or words of approval or disapproval. Any visitors who wanted to see him at work had to be especially warned to accept this discipline, so as not to complicate the situation. Needless to say, in some instances mothers might themselves be anxious (for example, at the child wanting to pick up the spatula), and might betray their own feelings, giving Winnicott some clues as to their own relation to their baby.

The spatula attracts the baby – it shines, perhaps even rocks on the table. There follows a sequence of events which Winnicott describes as normal – variations, of course, might tell him about the baby's particular psychological position, and it is the psychological that interests him in the game more than the indications of locomotor development. The first stage is when the baby touches the spatula, and then waits, or withdraws his hand. (He always uses the male noun or pronoun unless he is describing a specific case.) The baby then looks at mother and Winnicott to see what their reaction is to his interest in the object. He calls this 'the period of hesitation'. The baby's body is still, although not rigid. No re-assurance is given, and gradually the infant's interest returns to the spatula. Next 'he becomes brave enough to let his feelings develop, and then the picture changes quite quickly'. In Stage 2 there are physical changes to the baby's mouth and tongue and he salivates. The spatula is put into his mouth and chewed: 'instead of expect-ancy and stillness there now develops self-confidence'. The spatula is now the baby's possession. He may bang it, making as much noise as he can, or hold it to Winnicott's or mother's mouth, and is pleased if they pretend to be fed by it. 'He definitely wishes us to *play* at being fed, and is upset if we should be so stupid as to take the thing into our mouths and spoil the game as a game.'

Stage 3 is when the baby drops the spatula, 'as if by mistake'. If it is given back to him he is pleased, and drops it again, this time less by mistake; and now drops it on purpose in a new game. The end of this phase is when the baby either gets on the floor with the spatula, or is bored by the game.

The spatula game is more than a diagnostic tool, although it is partly that, providing clues both to the psychological state of the child and to the relationship between mother and baby. Madeleine Davis sees the game as a transition in Winnicott's development from a medical model to a psychoanalytic model, where 'diagnosis and therapy can't be separated because ultimately they both consist in a finding of the self' (Davis, 1993: 55). In his article, Winnicott gives three examples of the game's effectiveness as a therapeutic tool, reflecting or enabling different forms of healthy breakthrough to take place in the session. In one case, for example, he describes a nine-month-old girl's fortnight's illness, in which earache was accompanied by secondary psychological illness in loss of appetite and complete cessation of handling objects at home. In the consultation with him she was acutely distressed at even seeing the spatula, and pushed it away; but in the last stage of her recovery, the child caught hold of the spatula, made 'furtive attempts to mouth it' and then 'suddenly braved it, fully accepted it into her mouth and dribbled saliva'. The change marked a consequent change at home where she handled and mouthed objects as she had done before her illness.

If the spatula is a type of transitional object for Winnicott, 'through paediatrics to psychoanalysis' (as the first set of collected papers is called), it is also a transitional object for the child. It could be a symbol of a breast, of a penis (depending upon whether it is associated more with mother or father) although Winnicott moves beyond such a psychoanalytically conventional explanation to suggest that the spatula also stands for 'a quality of mother, such as liveliness, punctuality at feed times, reliability and so on'. It stands for other people as whole persons as well as part objects. Above all it stands for the relationship between the baby and others, both the objective mother in the external world and her counterpart in his subjective mind, the internalized mother; and the game sometimes also reflects the baby's perception of the relationship between the mother and Winnicott, in turn standing for father and mother. Through the spatula game (and of course other games at home) 'the child revises his relations with things and people both inside and outside himself'.

The Squiggle

In his consultations with older children (again in the context of his clinics) Winnicott developed another game. The fullest descriptions of the squiggle game are in a series of case studies of children and adolescents ranging from 21 months to sixteen years, in *Therapeutic Consultations in Child Psychiatry* (1971b). The youngest patient with whom he uses squiggles is five years old. Apart from the significance of the squiggles again as both a diagnostic and a therapeutic tool, Winnicott's use of the interaction with the parents is a particularly valuable part of the case descriptions. The case of 'Alfred' provides a clear summary of the game and its use, and of the incorporation into the therapy of interviews with a parent. All references in this section unless otherwise stated are to that case (1971b: 110–26).

In this instance Winnicott has paper on the table between him and his young patient. He suggests a game, in which Winnicott first makes a squiggle (a free flowing continuous line) on the paper, which the child can turn into something. Then the child makes a squiggle, which Winnicott turns 'into something, and so the game develops. A game without rules.'

Alfred was ten years old. Winnicott saw him just the once, as well as seeing his mother for a further appointment. He was brought because of his stammering, which was not cured, but which the squiggle game threw light upon. Winnicott had only seventy minutes to work with Alfred, having obtained his mother's permission first. Winnicott's early questions about Alfred's father and his father's work brought on the stammering, so Winnicott turned to drawing, and the rest of the time passed with practically no stammering.

Alfred turned Winnicott's first squiggle into a face. 'I noticed while he was doing this rather deliberate work that every time he breathed out *he made a little push with his breath* . . . Eventually I talked about it with him and it proved to be a significant feature' (Winnicott's italics). Alfred's squiggle was one which Winnicott turned into a man's bow tie. Winnicott's second squiggle Alfred turned into two balloons, saying 'That's all I can do' – as if more was expected of him, although the significance of this was not yet clear. With two or so more squiggles Alfred became more at ease, and was 'rather pleased' when Winnicott turned Alfred's third squiggle into a road sign, 'a sort of super-ego symbol'. Winnicott observes that his own conversions of squiggles are not done deliberately, but just on the basis of what occurs to him from seeing the squiggle. The therapist, like the young patient, follows wherever the unconscious leads.

As he explains, one of the aims of the game is to put the child at ease, and reach into the child's fantasy and dreams. Winnicott began to talk to Alfred about dreams, which gave rise to an excited response as the boy drew a squiggle with his right hand (he was normally left-handed) that Winnicott turned into a witch. He was dismayed a few minutes later when Alfred spoke about a dream of witches, lest he had influenced him, but he was re-assured by the boy that this was not the case. There followed more drawings and dreams and talking about the child's past at about the time of the witch dream, when Alfred was six and a half, at the same time that the family moved for his father to take up new work. Winnicott referred also to Alfred's 'breathing tension . . . pushing with his breath', which Alfred recognized and which led on to his talking about his stammer – another example of 'trying hard' and having to make an effort to speak. Similarly he had been trying hard in school. Winnicott linked this to passing faeces although 'it took a long time for us to get a common language here. The word "shit" was no good. Eventually we reached the family term "go to the lavatory".' Alfred said he would like to stop trying hard, and drew a squiggle which he converted himself, into a man with a violin case with a strap around it: his father played the violin.

The hour was up, and Winnicott then saw Alfred's mother. He said to her, 'I am sure that we must get to what happened when this boy was 6½,' upon which mother said, 'Did he tell you that at that time his father had a mental breakdown? You see, his father found his new job exacting, and he got caught up in a tremendous effort to succeed.' Winnicott had three minutes left, so he asked to see Alfred again and told him of the conversation he had just had with his mother. Asking Alfred whether he remembered his father's breakdown, Alfred was taken aback, and said he had completely forgotten it; but he also looked 'immensely relieved'. Winnicott said, 'You see you've been trying all this time, not because of your own need to try, and you have told me that things go better if you don't try. *You've been trying hard on your father's account,* and you are still going on trying to cure father of this worry about his work . . . it's this pushing and trying that interferes with all your work and your talking, and that makes you stutter.'

Winnicott makes it clear, at the start of this case study, that his consultation with Alfred did not cure the stammer, although it clearly eased it. Two months after this interview Winnicott saw Alfred's mother for an hour, and learned more of the compulsive behaviour Alfred had shown in the anal stage of his development, with mother finding herself constantly telling him to relax. But the stammer had started around the time his father was hospitalized with his depression. The mother reported an improvement. She said that Alfred had responded well to the interview: he told her as he left it that he had completely forgotten the time when his daddy was ill; and a few weeks later, he referred to Winnicott, saying 'That doctor was bang-on.' Yet his mother also reported how Alfred had begun to improve a week before the consultation; 'in fact, it started the moment I knew I was coming to see you'. Winnicott comments that 'it is quite usual for symptomatic improvement to be related to the mother's or the father's change-over from hopeless bewilderment to hopefulness'. Other case studies in *Therapeutic Consultations* illustrate similarly the importance of simultaneously working with parents – in one, for example, it was helping a mother that enabled her to accept her true role as the ill person in the mother–child couple, so that she stopped using the daughter as the ill one (Case XVIII, Mrs X). What is strange in the more extensive case study of the Piggle (see below) is that Winnicott does not record linking the little girl's mother's stated anxieties and issues about sibling rivalry with her daughter's presenting problems. In that case, as in his hospital clinic, his contact with parents (either at the same time or in a separate interview) is in marked distinction from Melanie Klein, his one-time supervisor, whose technique demands that parents be excluded from the consultation and indeed, inasmuch as they are regarded as significant internal objects rather than as external reality, from the therapy itself.

What Winnicott additionally demonstrates in the case of Alfred is the way in which the parents' issues can impinge upon their child, so that the child carries the pathology of the parent on her or his behalf – another crucial reason for seeing the mother and/or father as well. The last squiggle Alfred drew – significantly his own creation from start to finish – well illustrates how the child's symptoms can reflect the concerns of others. It was as if he was saying – through the squiggle of father and his violin with a strap around it – that father was unable to develop his musical interest. If Alfred could undo the strap, father might then become creative and make contact with a deeper self. If father were happier, Alfred might be able to give up pushing and straining. Winnicott did not realize all this at the time, but it made sense to him later. In fact it was helping the 'recovery of the memory of his father's illness that produced the required effect'. And if a seven-year follow-up showed Alfred as a well balanced young man, Winnicott is realistic about the part he himself played. 'It is not my claim, of course, that the one interview produced all this, which is a mixture of the boy's growth process and of the family provision and management. But when he came to see me he did need help, and he got it.'

A final example from Winnicott's paediatric clinic further illustrates the key role he assigned to parents. 'When parents can be used they can work with great economy, especially if the fact is kept in mind that there will never be enough psychotherapists to treat all those in need of treatment' (1965b: 157). In a paper on 'String: a Technique of Communication' (1965b: 153–7) Winnicott records seeing a seven-year-old boy because of a series of symptoms such as a compulsion to lick things, compulsive throat noises, and issues around defecation. From the parents he learned that the boy had experienced a number of separations from his mother due to another pregnancy when he was three, her admission to hospital for an operation, her depression, and her psychiatric admission. In playing the squiggle game with the boy, Winnicott noted that nearly everything he did was translated by the boy into something to do with string – a lasso, whip, crop, yo-yo string, string in a knot, etc. He asked the parents about the boy's preoccupation with string. They confirmed that he was obsessed with it, joining furniture together with strings, and recently tying a string around his young sister's neck.

Winnicott's opportunities were limited. He knew they could only see him once every six months because of distance. He therefore explained to the boy's mother that her son was concerned about the fear of separation, attempting to deny it by using string. She was sceptical of this explanation, but Winnicott asked her to broach the subject with the boy at a convenient time, 'letting him know what I said, and then developing the theme of separation according to the boy's response' (1965b: 154–5).

Six months later he saw the family again. Although the boy's mother had thought it silly, she had opened the subject of separation with her son, and found him keen to talk about his relationship with her. The string play ceased following that conversation; and although it showed itself again at various times, it was invariably related to fears of separation, and stopped as soon as the concern could be voiced. On another occasion (some years later) father had noticed the boy hanging upside down on a rope in the garden, acting as if dead. 'The father realized he must take no notice' (1965b: 156) staying close but getting on with other jobs for half an hour, until the boy got bored and stopped the game. 'This was a big test of the father's lack of anxiety,' comments Winnicott, in a phrase reminiscent of his advice to social workers not to be frightened or overcome with guilt when their clients behave in a bizarre fashion: 'if you can hold the situation together the possibility is that the crisis will resolve itself' (1965b: 229). In this case, although Winnicott believed that he had helped the mother to deal with the boy's use of string 'just before it was too late, when the use of it still contained hope' (1965b: 157), he nevertheless suggests that the preoccupation could turn into a perversion.

Winnicott's creativity both as a paediatrician and as a child therapist is seen in the inventiveness with which he employs the spatula, the squiggle, and in this last example the imagery of string. In this inventive therapeutic attitude he is of course not unique. Hobson (1985: 10–15) similarly uses drawings built up from an initial wavy line, in his case to break through the impasse of non-communication; and he too employs the terms 'play' and 'space' in describing the interaction with his patients. Similar though his examples of drawings in his book on conversational therapy may appear to be, Hobson notes (1985: 283) that he did not at the time know of Winnicott's use of squiggles. Winnicott's capacity to use such simple yet revealing approaches to communication well illustrates what Hobson writes: 'a psychotherapist needs to learn to play many different "language-games"' (1985: 15).

The Piggle

Winnicott's adaptation of technique meant that while in some cases analysis with children would be regular, at other times it was on demand: sometimes single and sometimes more frequent consultations. In the case of the Piggle, for example, the sixteen consultations extended over thirty months. Such flexibility may be less divergent from analytic technique than at first appears, because he also states that a child should be seen either on demand or daily – 'once a week treatments . . . are of doubtful value' (1980: 3). Winnicott explains that child analysis can never be complete, because the normal developmental processes take over as the analysis itself begins to show results. Some improvement at the outset may result from the analysis, but in time 'it is difficult to distinguish between clinical improvement and emotional development, between work done in the treatment and the maturational processes that have now become freed' (1980: 2). It is almost a case of necessary but minimal intervention, since treatment has disadvantages as well as advantages in the developmental process: 'It is possible for the treatment of a child actually to interfere with a very valuable thing which is the ability ɔf the child's home to tolerate and to cope with the child's clinical states that indicate emotional strain and temporary holdups in emotional development, or even the fact of development itself' (1980: 2).

Gabrielle ('the Piggle' as her parents affectionately called her) was two years and four months old when her parents first approached Winnicott in 1964. Because the family lived a long way from London, it was impossible for Winnicott to see Gabrielle for regular analysis. Instead it was arranged 'on demand', in practice every one or two months, when Gabrielle in one way or another (either by asking or by her symptoms) made it clear she wanted to see him. Her parents were professional people, who understood something of analysis. They listened to and observed Gabrielle carefully and sensitively, and communicated regularly between sessions with Winnicott. They obviously considered full analysis for the Piggle, but could not afford to move to London. Winnicott at one time even half suggested this – although, as he admits, he was partly confused in this suggestion by having a student who wanted a case. There were sixteen consultations in all spread over two and a half years. 'The fact that the sessions were "on demand" in no way altered the fact that the child was having an analysis' (1980: 73n).

Gabrielle had reacted in a florid way to the birth of her baby sister when she was 21 months old. She developed fears and fantasies, about a black mummy and daddy – the black mummy living in her tummy and often being ill. She appeared not to have an identity of her own: she was either the baby or the mummy. Part of the fantasy involved a 'babacar' (her name for the new baby) and a black Piggle. Her behaviour included finding it difficult to get to sleep at night, anxiety about her mother's breasts, and regressing in wanting to suck her mother's breasts. Some of the parents' comments give the impression that they might have been more anxious than they need have been, since, as Winnicott says, Gabrielle's 'thoughts and worries' were probably not untypical of 'a great number of children', obviously related to being pushed out by a new arrival. Indeed, the Piggle's mother in her first letter to Winnicott suggests that their own anxiety about the age gap before having a second child contributed to 'a great change in her' (1980: 6). As I noted above, he makes no use of this in his work with Gabrielle, at least as far as his record goes, even when her mother reveals (in a letter to him following the twelfth consultation) that she (the mother) had been intensely anxious at the time of her second child's birth; and that she herself had greatly resented her brother's birth. She was then almost exactly the same age as Gabrielle was when her sister was born (1980: 161).

What Winnicott does observe to the parents is that Gabrielle's worries 'are not usually so well verbalized, and this in Piggle's case has a lot to do with your both being particularly conscious of childhood matters and tolerant of childhood questions' (1980: 74–5). His work with her was primarily that of encouraging the natural maturational process. As he wrote to the mother after the fifth consultation: 'It is much better to think in terms of natural recovery, with an occasional visit to me helping things along a bit. The Piggle is a very interesting child, as you know. You might prefer that she were not so interesting, but there it is, and I expect that she will settle down into being quite ordinary soon' (1980: 74).

The case-notes of his consultations with the Piggle tell us much about the way Winnicott worked and the way he thought. Play is clearly central to his approach. He describes the Piggle's 'face play' in the second consultation: 'She moved her tongue around; I imitated, and so we communicated about hunger and tasting and mouth noises, and about oral sensuality in general' (1980: 25). He encouraged the Piggle to play with toys and with the doll she brought with her, observed her playing with her father ('she went over to daddy and started to use him, and I pulled back the curtain that hid him so that he was more part of the toy situation' (1980: 43). Play becomes a means of controlling her situation 'so that she was playing at it rather than being in it'. We see Winnicott playing too, including play-acting: firstly in being Gabrielle so that he expresses what she might be feeling; secondly referring to himself as a focus for her inner world through her projecting it on to him; thirdly playing at being the bad mother whom Gabrielle fantasizes as the black mummy, and identifies with as the black Piggle.

An example of the first type of play appears in the second consultation:

Me: I want to be the only baby. I want all the toys.
Piggle: You've got all the toys.
Me: Yes, but I want to be the only baby; I don't want there to be any more babies . . . I want to be the only baby [and, in a different voice], shall I be cross?
Piggle: Yes.

(1980: 29)

At this point Winnicott made a big noise and knocked over the toys, repeating forcefully that he wanted to be the only baby. This appeared both to please Gabrielle and also slightly to frighten her. Soon afterwards in her game she said 'I want to be the baby too.' Winnicott plays a similar role (i.e. Gabrielle) in the third consultation when Winnicott says to the Piggle, 'I wanted daddy to give me a baby', to which Gabrielle responds by saying to her father, 'Will you give Winnicott a baby?' Later in the same session a different example is seen, in Gabrielle's projection on to Winnicott as she says to him: 'Be a Winnicott. Daddy will look after you. Will you Daddy? If I close the door, Winnicott will be frightened' (1980: 44–5). The third type of play-acting, this time partly in the role of mother, is seen when Winnicott says to Gabrielle: 'The black mummy is now Winnicott and he is going to send the Piggle away' (1980: 61). This last remark is in fact right at the end of the fourth session, and Winnicott comments (to the reader), 'I stayed where I was being the black angry mummy *who wanted to be daddy's little girl and was jealous of Gabrielle*. At the same time I was Gabrielle being jealous of the new baby with mother' (1980: 61, Winnicott's italics).

Notice how Winnicott normally refers to himself in the third person when he talks to Gabrielle. Names are clearly important to him, since he considers at what point he should change from calling her the Piggle to using her real name. He wants to match her transition into finding her own identity, as the theme of me/not-me is introduced into the therapy, and Gabrielle clearly confirms to her mother that he gets it exactly right (1980: 84). By the sixth consultation he is using her name, and clarifying the distinction between them: 'Gabrielle and Winnicott make friends, but still Gabrielle is Gabrielle and Winnicott is Winnicott' (1980: 78). There is also a very significant point in the thirteenth session where Gabrielle first addresses him as Mr Winnicott, which Winnicott takes up as 'You can be a mender so you don't need me as a mender now. So I am Mr. Winnicott' (1980: 166). This is a much more conventional interpretation, at a time towards the end of therapy when communication between them is much more conversational and 'adult'. Indeed in the penultimate session Winnicott emphasizes the reality of the situation to Gabrielle as they prepare to finish. 'Yes, I am a doctor, and I could be Susan's doctor [her baby sister] but the Winnicott that you invented is finished forever' (1980: 190).

What Winnicott has done is to provide himself, as well as the toys in his consulting room, as an object to be played with. He has been a transitional object himself. He also permits the child to use whichever of her parents is present as part of play, often as objects or play assistants, helping her physically act out her fantasies – father helps her to go through 'being born' from between his legs. In a commentary on the thirteenth session, Winnicott writes of the need for a child to play and enjoy games first of all, if they are to get any meaning out of them. 'As a matter of principle, the analyst always allows the enjoyment to become established before the content of the play is used for interpretation' (1980: 175).

There is a clear progression through the sessions (with some temporary regressions), and a shift in Winnicott's own responses in parallel with Gabrielle's own development. To some extent the changes in her are made more obvious by the intervals between sessions in which Gabrielle was going through her own natural maturational processes, although her parents report significant points of change in the little girl following most sessions. At the start Winnicott's conversation reflects her regressed state and, though clearly to us symbolic, is nevertheless much more literal than metaphorical, and hardly ever interpretative. At one point in his notes on the third session he writes: 'Importance of my not *understanding* what she had not yet been able to give me clues for. Only she knew the answers, and when she could encompass the meaning of the fears she would make it possible for me to understand too' (1980: 48, Winnicott's italics). His choice of words is careful, reflecting her own: at one point he admits a mistake in using 'breasts' rather than 'yams' which is the Piggle's term. It is only later, in the child's own time, that their conversation becomes more reflective and interpretative. In the fourth session, for example, he describes how 'I made a rather definite interpretation to do with her wanting daddy all to herself so that mummy turns black, which means angry' (1980: 60). He notes that after this session she showed signs of coming out of regression and becoming a much more grown-up girl. At that time pleasure in playing, rather than compulsive playing, was more obvious, bearing out his observation that interpretation can only follow real pleasure in play. In the twelfth session he notes how he 'started to play about with interpretations' (1980: 155), and he makes what appear to be a good many of them, including her anger with him for not always being hers.

I refer here to spoken interpretations: Winnicott's notes throughout the case certainly contain allusions to psychoanalytic (especially Kleinian) interpretations of the material, as he refers briefly to her fantasies about intercourse and birth, to indications of oral, anal and sexual sadism, to urethral eroticism and clitoral excitement, to part-objects, etc. He shows how he toys with several interpretations as in the sixth consultation she puts carriages of a train together, and (differing from what Klein would have done) opts for accepting Gabrielle's own interpretation about making friends rather than his own suggestion about their making babies. The interpretations Winnicott makes, whether to Gabrielle or in his private comments, in no way obscure the centrality of the relationship he has with her, which stands out as being free from both jargon and the super-imposition of theoretical ideas.

Therapy is about the provision of the conditions that will foster the natural (if delayed) processes of maturation. In the thirteenth session with Gabrielle, Winnicott lists (with her) the different roles he has with her: 'the mending Winnicott and the cooking Winnicott . . . the teaching Winnicott . . . the play Winnicott' (1980: 174–5), to which she later adds the Winnicott who has to clear up after the session. This modest although essential view of the part the therapist has to play in the therapeutic process is typical of other situations, such as in the case of Alfred above, or in residential care. Here again, therapeutic provision is not confined to the consulting room. The family also provides it; or, as quoted in Chapter 1 from his lecture on 'Residential care as therapy', he soon learned as a visiting psychiatrist to a wartime hostel for evacuation failures that 'the therapy was being done by the walls and the roof; by the glass conservatory which provided a target for bricks; by absurdly large baths . . . by the cook, by the regularity of the arrival of food on the table, by the warm enough and perhaps warmly coloured bedspreads' (1984: 221).

Holding and Containment

Winnicott's therapeutic work with adults is, as one would expect, intimately linked to his understanding of childhood experiences and his work as a child psychotherapist. Whereas with children he sees his role as providing a means for their natural developmental processes to take place, in the case of those who are already adult patients it is different. The developmental processes through their childhood have not been straightforward, and may have resulted in an adaptation known as the 'false self' (see pp. 58–9 above). Winnicott regards what many lay people experience as a 'break-down' as potentially a healthy sign, implying both the capacity of and the opportunity for an individual to use the resources that are now available to them (internal as well as external), 'to re-establish an existence on a basis that feels real' (1965b: 225).

In a paper on aspects of regression within the psychoanalytic setting (1975: 278-94) Winnicott separates analytic cases into three categories, observing that analysts, by carefully selecting (quite appropriately) those whom they choose to treat, 'usually . . . avoid meeting aspects of human nature that must take us beyond our natural equipment' (1975: 278). The first and most common group of patients are those who 'operate as whole persons and whose difficulties are in the realm of interpersonal relationships' (1975: 279). For these patients classical psychoanalysis is the appropriate technique. The second group of patients are those 'in whom wholeness of the personality only just begins to be something that can be taken for granted' (1975: 279). Here analysis has to do with the events that belong to the achievement of wholeness, such as the coming together of love and hate – what Kleinians call 'the depressive position'. 'These patients require the analysis of mood' (1975: 279). Technique is not very different from that with the first category, although there may be new management problems because of the increased range of material tackled: 'important from our point of view here is the idea of the *survival of the analyst* as a dynamic factor' (1975: 279, Winnicott's italics). The third group consists of patients in whom the analysis must deal with the earliest stages of emotional development, before the establishment of the whole personality, and before the achievement of distinctions of space, time and status. 'The accent is more surely on management, and sometimes over long periods with these patients ordinary analytic work has to be in abeyance, management being the whole thing' (1975: 279).

Winnicott's paper is mainly about working with this group: indeed it is perhaps the analysis of patients who are in one way or another (using Winnicott's definition) 'regressed' that is the most original contribution in his various papers on 'technique'. 'Technique' is not quite the right term, since Winnicott himself says that there is a difference between technique and treatment: 'it is possible to carry through treatment with limited technique, and it is possible with highly developed technique to fail to carry through a treatment' (1975: 279). Classical psychoanalytic technique had of course already been fully explored – there was little new to add to it. Winnicott's distinctive contribution was to the treatment and management of those in his second and third categories of patient. He also writes elsewhere about working with those in whom early environmental damage or failure gives rise to a rather different presentation, antisocial behaviour. But here I concentrate upon his identification of those features which are necessary for working with those who present a state of internal chaos, rather than demonstrate external destructiveness.

By 'regression' Winnicott does not mean simply the appearance of infantile behaviour, which is its popular meaning. He refers rather to regression as 'the reverse of progress', and as 'a highly organized ego-defence mechanism, one which involves the existence of a false self' (1975: 281). He also refers to a 'caretaker self' defending against early environmental failure by 'freezing the failure situation' (1975: 281), in the hope that there will be an opportunity of its unfreezing, through a present-day environment that can foster 'adequate though belated adaptation' (1975: 283). True to his assertion that technique is not the same as treatment, Winnicott believes that there can be spontaneous recovery from psychosis, whereas recovery from neurosis needs a psychoanalyst. Although Winnicott does not say it here, his willingness to share his insights with other therapeutic professions suggests that he might also include other specialist helpers alongside analysts as playing their own part in working with neurosis. But he makes a clear distinction about psychosis, that it 'is closely related to health, in which innumerable environmental situations are frozen but are reached and unfrozen by the various healing phenomena of ordinary life, namely friendships, nursing during physical illness, poetry, etc.' (1975: 284).

It is therefore not surprising to find Winnicott addressing social workers ('The Mentally Ill in your Caseload', 1965b: 217–29) and setting out principles for the social worker as a therapist: 'but not . . . the kind of therapist who makes the correct and well-timed interpretation' that is typical of work with neurotic patients (1965b: 227). His advice clearly reflects the way he saw his own role as a therapist working with deeply disturbed patients. In therapy of this kind the function of the therapist is the same as that of parents who seek to correct 'relative failures in environmental provision . . . they exaggerate some parental function and keep it up for a length of time, in fact until the child has used it up and is ready to be released from special care' (1965b: 227).

The therapist is not at all providing a corrective experience. For a start no-one can create a corrective transference experience, because the transference is dictated by the patient's unconscious processes and not by the good intentions of the analyst. It is however possible that *good technique* may provide a corrective experience, such as therapy proving to be the first occasion a patient gets the full attention of another person for fifty minutes, or their first experience of reliability, or of someone being objective. But it is never enough. What Winnicott more assuredly states *is* enough for some patients to get well is that 'in the end the patient uses the analyst's failures, often quite small ones', some of which will have been 'manoeuvred' by the patient. The key factor is that the patient is then able to hate the analyst for the failure, originally experienced in an early environmental failure, but now repeated in the transference. 'In the end we succeed by failing – failing the patient's way' (1965b: 258).

The therapist (and the social worker in this type of casework) is a 'human basket' into which clients put all their eggs, testing out to see if the therapist will be sensitive and reliable, or will repeat the traumatic experiences of the past. Another image he uses is the frying pan 'with the frying process played backwards, so that you really do unscramble the scrambled eggs' (1965b: 227). Such care, like infant care itself, consists of holding and containing. It starts as a simple process, but similarly becomes complex. Its aim is not to direct growth, but to provide an environment in which natural tendencies at work in the individual can be encouraged: 'a natural evolution based on growth'. One of the complications is that if the therapist is able to provide this reliable holding environment, clients or patients may become more ill, because there is now some hope of healing the deeper parts of the self. 'Your client uses your special provision in order to become disintegrated or uncontrolled or dependent in the way that belongs to the period of infancy . . . The client goes mad' (1965b: 228).

When this happens (when the client goes mad), as I have already referred to above, the therapist (and psychiatric social worker) is enjoined not to be frightened or overcome with guilt. This comforting thought (if at the same time impossible ideal!) is one of a number of key principles which Winnicott sets out for those who work with regressed clients, and which obviously lie at the heart of his own experience of patients who entered and lived through such a psychotic state. I quote just a few of his guidelines:

> You get to know what it feels like to be your client.
> You become *reliable* for the limited field of your professional responsibility. . . .
> You accept love, and even the in-love state, without flinching and without acting-out your response.
> You accept hate and meet it with strength rather than with revenge.
> You tolerate your client's illogicality, unreliability, suspicion, muddle, fecklessness, meanness, etc. etc., and recognize all these unpleasantnesses as symptoms of distress.
>
> (1965b: 229)

The context for which this advice was written appears to confine it to working with the most disturbed people. What lies behind each phrase, however, is a view of the interaction between parent and child that refers not simply to the earliest levels of disturbance, but also to more normal situations, such as in adolescence. For example, in his talk on adolescence (published in both 1971a and 1986) Winnicott speaks to parents of their children needing to find 'the whole of themselves, and that will include the aggression and destructive elements in themselves as well as the elements that can be labelled loving. There will be this long tussle which you will need to survive' (1971a: 143); and that in relation to adolescents in particular, 'parents can help only a little; the best they can do is to *survive*, to survive intact, and without changing colour, without relinquishment of any important principle' (1971a: 145, Winnicott's italics).

The theme of 'surviving' stands out throughout Winnicott's writing on good practice, whether it is as a therapist or a parent. This would appear therefore to argue that therapists working at all levels could benefit from the guidance given to those who work with the most florid of cases, certainly along the lines quoted above. Nevertheless, when working with psychotic anxieties and behaviour, particular variations in standard analytic practice appear to be essential in order to help the patient to survive.

Winnicott's papers are particularly helpful and memorable for their 'lists': shorthand summaries that encapsulate his thinking about a subject, but that are not always further developed. The list of guidelines for social workers is one example; on p. 88 I draw on a very perceptive list of the reasons why a mother hates her baby. In the paper on 'Metapsychological and Clinical Aspects of Regression' (1975: 278-94) there are several such summaries in Winnicott's inimitable style, one of which lists features of the classical psychoanalytic setting. For example:

2.   The analyst would be there, on time, alive, breathing.
9.   In the analytic situation the analyst is much more reliable than people are in ordinary life; on the whole punctual, free from temper tantrums, free from compulsive falling in love, etc.

(1975: 285)

Reliability is also listed amongst the steps involved in working with regression, a summary which merits further study for the reader who is particularly interested in this side of Winnicott's practice (1975: 286–7). Analysis in this case 'reproduces the early and earliest mothering techniques. It invites regression by reason of its reliability. The regression of a patient is an organized return to early dependence. . .'. There is a sequence of events in regression, from confidence in the setting, through regression to dependence, feeling a new sense of self, unfreezing the environmental failure, feeling and expressing anger in the present setting that is related to the early environmental failure, the return from regression to dependence, and then to independence, and finally realizing needs and wishes with vitality and vigour. The linear sequence is, however, a little deceptive because 'all this is repeated again and again' (1975: 287).

If Winnicott's summaries encapsulate his thought and practice, my own summary scarcely does justice to this rich area of writing, since space does not permit me the opportunity to record many other significant features. For example, he lists how to respond to acting out. He makes it clear that he is totally against *encouraging* patients to regress – to do so demonstrates gross pathology in the analyst. Regression can only result from the patient's initiative (albeit a partly unconscious move). His proposals concerning this aspect of a therapist's work do not, he says, affect the principles of ordinary practice (although, as I show below through evidence of his own 'ordinary practice' this is a little questionable). Finally, working in this way is very obviously something he does not recommend in the first decade of practice (1975: 293).

In the course of this centrally important paper Winnicott refers to 'one of my patients who has perhaps taught me most about regression' (1975: 279). The unidentified patient we now know to be Margaret Little, who has written her own account of her breakdown and regression (1985; 1990), and of her analysis with Winnicott. It is the fullest first-hand record we have of his style as a therapist in such situations, complementing his descriptions of the role of the analyst in such treatment settings.

Little describes how in one early session, in despair of ever getting him to understand her (despite a first meeting where he clearly picked up a theme which had been totally neglected in her two previous analyses with other therapists) she

> attacked and smashed a large vase filled with white lilac, and trampled on it. In a flash he was gone from the room, but he came back just before the end of the hour. Finding me clearing up the mess he said, 'I might have expected you to do that [clear up? or smash?] but later.' Next day an exact replica had replaced the vase and the lilac, and a few days later he explained that I had destroyed something that he valued. (1990: 43)

There is much more in this than just surviving, although the replica vase perhaps symbolizes that. We may wonder why Winnicott left the room so quickly, and only returned at the end of the hour. It is curious, as Little herself says, that neither of them ever referred to the incident again. She thinks that 'if it had happened later on he would probably have behaved differently'; later in her account she explains: 'D. W. was not yet ready to meet this destructive acting-out and left me alone with the chaos I had created, so the sense of futility and hopelessness remained' (1990: 96). Yet Winnicott 'a few days later' revealed some of his feelings about the vase if not about the incident, and years later, after the analysis had finished, he agreed with Little that she had hurt him 'but added that it has been "useful"' (1990: 43). Showing his own feelings, whether of anger or pleasure, is also apparent in other accounts of his interactions with patients. Surviving is not the same as being passive. Not retaliating is different from not responding.

The degree of terror that Margaret Little experienced is clear from her account. Extremely anxious at first, she put off his preliminary offer to see her, but he 'said he would keep the vacancy open for the time being'. She was soon back, but in the first session 'lay curled up tight, completely hidden under the blanket, unable to move or speak. D. W. was silent until the end of the hour, when he said only, "I don't *know*, but I have the feeling that you are shutting me out for some reason"' (1990: 42). The low key, almost obvious, but hesitant response brought her relief, because he admitted not knowing; and in fact later she reflected on that time as her shutting herself in rather than shutting him out. The terror surfaced again and again. She records a time when she 'grabbed his hands and clung tightly till the spasms had passed. He said at the end that he thought I was reliving the experience of being born; he held my head for a few minutes' (1990: 43). As he explained, a baby's head after birth aches and feels heavy (and, we might add, for some weeks after birth needs always to be supported). To Little the session was like 'birth *into a relationship*' (1990: 44, her italics), and for many sessions after that she describes him as holding her two hands clasped in his.

Such holding and containing is for Winnicott of crucial import-ance in the practice of therapy. Most frequently 'holding' needs to be understood as metaphorical, as Little explains: 'holding the situation, giving support, keeping contact on every level with what-ever was going on, in and around the patient and in the relationship to him' (1990: 44). But for patients who were experiencing deep levels of disturbance, such holding was sometimes literal. Con-taining also involved delegating responsibility for patients at times when he was unable to see them – when he was ill, or on holiday. For example he arranged for a friend of Margaret Little to invite her when he was on holiday (without Little knowing), and at another break arranged for her to stay in hospital, in his words 'to make sure that I did not commit suicide' (1990: 58). Early in her analysis she was physically ill, and he came to her home, five, six or even seven days a week for ninety minutes each day, for about three months. 'During most of these sessions I simply lay there, crying, held by him' (1990: 52).

Such literal holding has to be seen in context. Whereas in the therapy of neurotic patients the therapist is seen as if he were mother or father, and employs the transference and transference interpretations as a way of containing and understanding the patient's responses and reactions, in psychosis the 'as if' becomes reality. So Little comments: 'To me D. W. did not *represent* my mother. In my transference delusion he actually *was* my mother. . . so to me his hands were the umbilical cord, his couch the placenta, and blanket the membranes, all far below any *conscious* level until a very late stage' (1990: 98, Little's italics. Winnicott writes similarly; see 1975: 288). Although Freud's injunction that the analyst should engage in free-floating attention is similar to Winnicott's phrase 'primary maternal preoccupation', the degree and the purpose of this attention are different. Little singles out 'treatment' as being the key to work with the psychotic, rather than technique, and intuition and management as being more important than interpretation (1990: 88). She records very few actual interpretations in Winnicott's responses. Rather, she describes him in different terms:

> I found D. W. essentially a truthful person, to whom 'good manners' were important; he had respect for the individual . . . though he could be outspoken in criticism. To demand 'associations' or to push an 'interpretation' would be 'bad manners', as well as being useless. He was as honest as anyone could be, responding to observations and answering questions truthfully unless there was a need to protect another person . . . He would answer questions directly, taking them at face value, and only then considering (always with himself, often with the patient) why it was asked? Why then? And what was the unconscious anxiety behind it? (1990: 47)

Little later recalls that while he did not talk with her about his depression at the break-up of his marriage (even though she was well aware of it from his appearance and manner) 'eventually he told me of his divorce and coming remarriage, lest I should hear of it elsewhere' (1990: 55).

There are dangers in taking such selections from Little's moving account of Winnicott. It is important to remember that he had had twenty years of experience of seeing psychotic patients before he saw her, and that even then, as I have indicated already, mistakes were inevitable. There were things he missed or misunderstood; but inevitably so, because no-one can ever give to another all that the other wants; and it is through mistakes that the therapist makes it clear that perfection is a useless and impossible desire. As he said of the job of parenting, 'Perfection has no meaning' (1984: 108). It is essential to remember that he held patients back from this type of regression, as already cited: 'the timing of the full regression could not be mine alone: it depended to a large extent on his case load' (Little, 1990: 47). While he gave more of himself than might be expected of a therapist, he also 'made it clear that total self-sacrifice was just not on. If he did not care for himself, providing for his own needs, bodily and emotional, he would be of no use to anyone' (Little, 1990: 64).

Finally it is important to be reminded that this was psycho-analysis, not once-weekly psychotherapy and counselling, and that even then it lasted over seven years. Seductive though this degree of involvement may be to the counsellor or therapist who longs to enter into deep therapeutic relationships, Little's account has to be read with the recognition that such work was not Winnicott's norm (even if it was clearly a constant dimension to his practice). It was risky: Winnicott records the 'disastrous effect' of speaking his mind with a different patient in his paper 'Hate in the Counter-Transference' (1975: 197–8); and although it concerned a Jungian analyst rather than a follower of Winnicott, the uncannily similar intensely close therapeutic relationship between Sarah Ferguson and Robert Moody, 'fictionalized' in A Guard Within (Ferguson, 1973) ended in the death of them both. Indeed, ironically, Ferguson's title reminds therapists and counsellors that their work requires their own guard within. In Winnicott we find clear recognition of the necessity both of closely observing the patient and of constantly and honestly monitoring the therapist's counter-transference (see below). Even so, such work surely must also have taken its toll on him.

Hate and the Counter-Transference

Winnicott is sometimes such an enchanting writer, and often conveys such an engaging personality, that it is tempting to imagine that it was a positive maternal transference by his patients to him that must have contributed so much to his apparent success as a therapist. I use the term 'apparent' because we have no real measure of how successful the majority of his or any other therapies are. Neither is writing about them an attempt on his part to claim efficacy. That Winnicott writes about his experience in such a beguiling way is not evidence in itself that he was (nor that he claimed to be) more or less successful than any other therapist. He occasionally refers to cases where things sometimes went disastrously wrong. In the light of later events and Masud Khan's fall from grace, it is only possible to speculate how thorough

Winnicott's analysis of him was. But then a completed analysis, like religious conversion, should *not* imply human perfection.

I have already drawn attention to the way that he himself is willing to grapple with the negative: his feelings in the incident of the vase that Little broke early in her analysis, and his references to the need for the patient to hate the therapist for failing. There is a rather different example in *The Piggle* of him drawing out Gabrielle's destructive feelings in connection with the ending of her therapy. In the penultimate consultation she took hold of the toy father figure and started to twist it, to a commentary: 'I'm twisting his legs . . . his arm . . . now his neck . . . now his head has come off.' As she did this, Winnicott cried 'Ow! Ow!', which pleased her greatly. She was needing to get rid of him, partly (so he interpreted) so that her baby sister could never have him either. She wanted Winnicott 'destroyed and made dead' (1980: 191). A little later in the session, sensing perhaps her anxiety at what she had done, he drew a picture of Gabrielle on a piece of paper; then he twisted its arms, legs and head, and asked her if it hurt. She laughed and said, 'No, it tickles' (1980: 191). He needed to demonstrate to her that she had both killed him off and yet not hurt him.

Winnicott writes that under normal conditions a therapist's hate is latent, although it is expressed in an acceptable way in ending sessions or ending therapy itself. It can of course also be part of the therapist's own counter-transference – part of her or his own agenda, that needs looking at apart from the actual patient. In working with some patients however, particularly psychotic or antisocial patients, it is very important for the therapist to be able to make contact with hate. This is for a number of reasons: a therapist needs to have reached deep into herself or himself in order to work with disturbed people; even if justified with some patients, hate needs to be identified, and kept for the right moment for it to be interpreted; and patients need to know when they have identified a therapist's feeling correctly: 'In certain stages of certain analyses the analyst's hate is actually sought by the patient, and what is then needed is hate that is objective. If the patient seeks objective or justified hate he must be able to reach it, else he cannot feel he can reach objective love' (1975: 199).

In one brief example in the paper on 'Hate in the Counter-Transference' Winnicott records a particular point in one therapy, following progress to a point where the patient had become 'lovable', when he realized that the patient's former

> unlikeableness has been an active symptom, unconsciously determined. It was indeed a wonderful day for me (much later on) when I could

actually tell the patient that I and his friends had felt repelled by him, but that he had been too ill for us to let him know. This was also an important day for him, a tremendous advance in his adjustment to reality. (1975: 196)

In a longer example Winnicott shows fewer qualms about speaking his mind, although this is clearly to prevent him acting out his hate. He recounts how in the Second World War he and his first wife had living with them, for 'three months of hell', an evacuee boy of nine: 'the most lovable and most maddening of children' (1975: 199–200). First they had problems with him running away, but this was replaced by his bringing his destructiveness into their home. This shift, writes Winnicott, 'engendered hate in me . . . Did I hit him? The answer is no, I never hit. But I should have had to have done so if I had not known all about my hate and if I had not let him know about it too.' At times of crisis Winnicott would take him by sheer force, without any anger or blame, and put him outside the front door. There was a bell for him to ring to be let back in again, and he knew that nothing would be said about what had happened. He learned to use the bell when he had recovered from his maniacal attack. Winnicott adds: 'The important thing is that each time, just as I put him outside the door, I told him something; I said that what had happened had made me hate him' (1975: 200).

We are told little more, except that the boy went on to an approved school, yet the 'deeply rooted relation to us has remained one of the few stable things in his life'. Expressing himself in this way was vital for Winnicott, because it enabled him to tolerate the situation 'without losing my temper and without every now and again murdering him' (1975: 200).

Similarly 'a mother has to be able to tolerate hating her baby without doing anything about it'. The baby needs the mother to be able to tolerate her hate if the baby is to tolerate his own hate, just as the psychotic cannot 'tolerate his hate of the analyst unless the analyst can hate him' (1975: 202). Winnicott's list of reasons why a mother hates her baby is another string of gems. As examples:

He is ruthless, treats her as scum, an unpaid servant, a slave . . . .
He tries to hurt her, periodically bites her, all in love . . . .
He is suspicious, refuses her good food, and makes her doubt herself, but eats well with his aunt.
After an awful morning with him she goes out, and he smiles at a stranger, who says, 'Isn't he sweet?'
If she fails him at the start she knows he will pay her out for ever.
(1975: 201)

Strictly speaking, Winnicott's descriptions of both a mother's hate and his own hate of the acting-out boy are not counter-transference. As he correctly observes in his later paper on the subject (1965b: 158–65), counter-transference is not the same as a reaction, and by implication self-disclosure is not the same as an interpretation. Once, he writes, 'I got hit by a patient. What I said is not for publication. It was not an interpretation but a reaction to an event. The patient came across the professional white line and got a little bit of the real me, and I think it felt real to her. But a reaction is not counter-transference' (1965b: 164). The lesson is salutary. His second paper on counter-transference continually stresses the professionalism of the therapist, the space between the analyst and the patient, and the difference between the role of the therapist and the same person in everyday life. If Winnicott refreshingly opens the windows of the sometimes dry and stuffy psychoanalytic world to the fullness of human experience in the therapist, he does not at the same time issue a licence just to be oneself.

A 'Very Personal Technique'

Despite the distinctions that must be drawn, following Winnicott himself (1975: 278-94), between the analysis of psychotic and neurotic patients, there is much that is common to his practice in both areas of therapy, as well as in his work in the other settings in which he was professionally engaged. This common ground is seen in his emphasis upon the recognition and use of counter-transference, particularly the importance of hate in the counter-transference; his insistence that therapy must provide a holding and a facilitating environment in which people are given the opportunity to grow; and his intense 'maternal preoccupation' with his patients. But although Margaret Little reminds us that in cases of neurosis Winnicott used the 'standard technique – interpreting the transference, concentration upon repressed oedipal material and the activity of the superego' (Little, 1990: 76), on the same page she rightly describes Winnicott as possessing a 'very personal technique'. It is that which I seek to identify here.

In *Holding and Interpretation* (1989a) there is much material for examining Winnicott's therapeutic manner, since he made full notes of the last six months of an analysis of a male patient, whom he had seen first as a young man, and then again twelve years later. In his introduction, his editor Masud Khan states that 'Winnicott was an indefatigable note-taker of his clinical encounters. Where he found the energy and the time is a mystery' (1989a: 14). When using the squiggle game he was able to make brief notes on the back of the drawings. But the notes in this case are clearly more extensive than usual. They are in the main paraphrases and summaries of what was said, with occasional verbatim remarks on both sides. Winnicott explains that 'my patient spoke slowly and deliberately, and what he said could be easily recorded; I chose a special moment to make records, one which I knew would be decisive for the analysis; and I actually wrote down what I said whether I was pleased or ashamed of it' (1989a: 7).

Khan wonders whether one of the reasons Winnicott chose to make notes in this case was to keep himself awake, because the patient was schizoid in his presentation, and sometimes psychologically withdrew in the midst of a session, which could make attending to him difficult. This is perhaps one of the most important theoretical features of the case, since it provides Winnicott with several examples of how a therapist can respond to a patient's withdrawal in the session. Such withdrawal (variously also described as boredom or even going to sleep) could easily be experienced as a defensive position in which the patient holds on to the self, but excludes the therapist. Winnicott, however, sees possibilities for changing this: if the therapist can hold the patient, the patient's withdrawal can shift into a temporary regression, that 'carries with it the opportunity for correction of inadequate adaptation-to-need in the past history of the patient'. In the withdrawn state nothing can be changed; but regression and dependency are much more 'profitable' (1989a: 192). Holding the patient means, as so often in Winnicott, not physically holding (except sometimes as we have seen where there is more permanent regression), but understanding the patient at a deep level, and showing 'that we do so by a correct and well-timed interpretation' (1989a: 192).

If this is the main feature of interest to Winnicott in his paper 'Withdrawal and Regression' (in 1975 and 1989a) and in his summary of the whole analysis, our own interest additionally focuses on extensive opportunities of glimpsing Winnicott at work. I call this 'glimpsing' because, full though it is, his account is not the same as a live session, and there is little of the 'novella' quality to it that we find in Freud's classic case histories. While the detail permits a closer view of Winnicott's responses and interpretations, the account inevitably lacks affect and the subtleties of rhythm, pause, timing, non-verbal communication, or even extraneous noise (although Winnicott refers at one stage to a noisy cocktail party next door and its lack of impact on the patient). It may be something to do with the patient, but the interaction scarcely comes as alive as any of Freud's cases in *Studies on Hysteria* (Freud and Breuer, 1895). It is not as vivid as Little's account of her analysis. Perhaps this is partly because the material itself is not highly charged, and partly because it is the last part of an analysis: we do not know all that has gone before. Reading the notes is like overhearing parts of a conversation about people we do not know. But the reader who wants to take a magnifying glass to Winnicott's technique will be amply rewarded. I select just a few examples to show something of the way in which Winnicott worked.

He refers to the transference frequently: most of his interventions relate to himself and his patient, linking what is going on between them to mother–child (and sometimes father–child) relationships. He sometimes uses psychoanalytic concepts about infant and child development – although these may be shorthand for the purposes of the notes. Where direct quotations are included we notice how Winnicott's language is less technical. For example, he may use an image to interpret as well as to explain:

> I now gave him a longer and more detailed description of the two possible reactions, the schizoid and the depressive (without using those terms). I spoke in terms of the buttons of the coat pulled at by the child . . . when he got the button the important thing was that he was satisfied, and therefore the button became unimportant . . . [Winnicott now quotes himself in full:] 'There is another possible reaction, which I mention because it is there in the analysis but you are not yet able to see it. This would be concerns about the coat that was now devoid of a button, and also concerns about the fate of the button.' (1989a: 31)

He asks few questions. Most of his interventions are confident statements, although he prefaces some of them with the phrase 'I think. . .'. It is difficult to ascertain whether he means 'I wonder' or 'I believe', although Little comments that he 'often spoke tentatively, or speculated' (1990: 48). Certainly he mentions in several places how he got it wrong: 'I made a new interpretation, stating that my previous one had obviously been wrong'; and a little later in the same session: 'I made another interpretation, which I had to withdraw because I could tell from the effect that it was wrong' (Winnicott, 1989a: 23). Towards the end of the analysis Winnicott says to his patient: 'You value my flexibility and my willingness to try things out as I go along' (1989a: 185). Khan also comments that Winnicott had a 'monumental capacity . . . to contain unknowing' (Winnicott 1989a: 15).

There is considerable evidence in both Little's and Guntrip's descriptions of their therapy with Winnicott of how still and silent he could be, and yet how attentive he was to their needs; but these notes reveal much more verbal interchange. But when he speaks there is little sign of the over-measured, anonymous, somewhat objective interpretation that is all too commonly associated with therapists who prefer to present themselves to their patients as a 'blank screen'. At one point he reminds his patient of the last half hour of the previous session, and says that there is one part he cannot remember. A little later it comes back to him and he appears to tell the patient straightaway what it was. He discloses his own experience of the relationship, as this extract (partly verbatim) shows:

> *Patient*: He thought that I ought to be able to show excitement along with his excitement . . .
>
> *Analyst*: I replied to this that I was indeed excited, although perhaps not as excited as he would be since I was also not so much in despair during his despair periods. I was in a position to see the thing as a whole.
>
> *Patient*: He continued on the theme of the analyst's ability to be excited at progress in patients and I said:
>
> *Analyst*: You can take it from me that I do this kind of work because I think it is the most exciting thing a doctor can do, and it is certainly better from my point of view when patients are doing well than when they are not.
>
> (1989a: 30)

There are one or two other surprises in the case-notes. Khan explains how Winnicott had first seen the patient as a young man, and that eight years after the termination of the first analysis, he wrote to the patient's mother to find out how he was going on. Some four years later the mother contacted Winnicott, and this led to the patient's return to him. Winnicott points out to the patient that it was no accident that he (Winnicott) had sought him out, rather than the other way round. He saw him three times a week, on Tuesday, Wednesday and Thursday one week and Monday, Tuesday and Friday the alternate week. Although this was no doubt because of the patient's professional commitments, Winnicott still has briefly to justify three times a week as still being analysis. Perhaps he perceives the analytic establishment as requiring such an *apologia*, and he seems obliged to give it.

The end of the analysis is very abrupt. Although Winnicott makes it quite clear that he would prefer his patient to go on seeing him, he also clearly accepts that it is his choice, and re-assures him that he can leave at such a point without the risk of further damage. Nevertheless the ending appears to happen within the space of two sessions. Although the patient wrote after six months to confirm the probable permanence of the ending and to thank him, fourteen years after the end of this second spell of analysis Winnicott once more sought the patient out, writing to ask him how he was: 'I'm at the age at which one looks back and wonders' (1989a: 13). In a brief reply to a long letter from his former patient,

Winnicott comments that he is 'impressed by the way you have used your life instead of perpetual psychotherapy' (1989a: 13). We are reminded in these interchanges of the close relationship which Freud also had with some of his patients (such as the Wolf-man) and how the real relationship between them survived the relinquishing of the transference relationship.

These intensely personal features in therapeutic relationships are seen again in Harry Guntrip's account of his analysis with Winnicott, which he contrasts with an earlier, lengthier analysis he had with W. R. D. Fairbairn, the Scottish analyst and an equally important figure in British psychoanalysis. Apart from their therapeutic style (Fairbairn was unusually orthodox in his technique for someone who was revolutionary in his theory), Guntrip experienced each man in the transference relationship in completely different ways. Fairbairn became Guntrip's dominating bad mother, while Winnicott became the good mother. If this is partly due to the workings of Guntrip's unconscious, it was obviously also based upon the stimulus that came from within the core personality of each of these major analysts. Winnicott, throughout Guntrip's account of him, adopts the position of the good-enough mother, partly of course through his primary maternal preoccupation with his patients, but also by interpreting himself in that role.

Guntrip travelled from Leeds to London for a couple of sessions once a month with Winnicott from 1962 to 1968 – 150 sessions in all. We note again, as with the Piggle, and the boy and his string, that Winnicott was well able to work psychoanalytically despite widely spaced sessions – there is no suggestion that he was having to water down the analysis, as some of his more orthodox colleagues might say (and indeed did think in connection with the Piggle). In Guntrip's case the monthly analysis with Winnicott must have been helped by the earlier period with Fairbairn, by Guntrip's own considerable insight and skill as a therapist himself, by his continuing self-analysis, and through his almost obsessional habit of recording every session with Winnicott in detail, and working on it in the space between.

This latter practice was one which Winnicott eventually interpreted as linked to Guntrip's early traumatic experience of his mother, to whom it had been impossible to relate following the effect on her of the death of Guntrip's younger brother. Guntrip records Winnicott as saying about Guntrip's continuous talking and compulsive hard-working in the sessions (and problems both with silence and over-work outside the sessions): 'You have to work hard to keep yourself in existence. You're afraid to stop acting, talking or keeping awake. You feel you might die in a gap like

Percy [his brother], because if you stop acting mother can't do anything . . . You're bound to fear I can't keep you alive, so you link up monthly sessions for me by your records. No gaps' (Guntrip, 1975: 152). Winnicott by contrast, it may be remembered from Chapter 1, had little anxiety about space and gaps.

Winnicott picked up Guntrip's anxiety in their very first session, spotting the key element in what would become the transference relationship. Guntrip had explained that his basic problem was a mother in his early life who failed to relate at all. It was only at the end of the session that Winnicott spoke: 'I've nothing particular to say yet, but if I don't say something, you may begin to feel I'm not here' (Guntrip, 1975: 152).

In Guntrip Winnicott was working with someone who was clearly neither psychotically disturbed nor *regressed*, although Guntrip had recognized that his regressed ego was *repressed*. Nevertheless Winnicott immediately intervened at the level of early developmental themes; not the later Oedipal themes that might be expected from reading his descriptions of analytic technique with patients who present neurotic symptoms. There is no reference to the paternal transference as again might be expected of the more orthodox Freudian stance. Winnicott (indeed like Fairbairn and Guntrip himself) is drawn towards early trauma and the maternal relationship. In the transference he not only interprets in terms of mother and infant, but also becomes the good mother, listening, attending, fully present, and never deliberately depriving (as some of his Kleinian colleagues would believe is an essential to the provocation of unconscious material). As Guntrip says of him; 'He became a good breast mother to my infant self in my deep unconscious, at the point where my actual mother had lost her maternalism and could not stand me as a live baby any more' (Guntrip, 1975: 153).

It is important to allow for Guntrip's own position as a colleague as well as a patient in reading his account of Winnicott's relationship with him. It is tempting to fasten upon his description of Winnicott outside the work of the session itself, and not to recognize that the greatest impact Winnicott made upon him was through the therapeutic rather than through the collegial relationship. However, Guntrip contrasts Fairbairn's consulting room with Winnicott's – the latter was 'simple, restful in colours and furniture, unostentatious, carefully planned, so Mrs Winnicott told me, by both of them, to make the patient feel at ease' (Guntrip, 1975: 149). He also contrasts their personal style: 'I would knock and walk in, and presently Winnicott would stroll in with a cup of tea in his hand and a cheery "Hallo", and sit on a small wooden chair by the couch . . . always at the end, as I departed he held out his hand for a friendly handshake' (Guntrip, 1975: 149). Guntrip could use the couch to lie down or sit up as he felt inclined.

It is difficult to know whether it was their common profession and therefore their more equal status that led Winnicott at one point to tell Guntrip his own feelings about him as a rather special patient: 'I'm good for you but you're good for me. Doing your analysis is almost the most reassuring thing that happens to me. The chap before you makes me feel I'm no good at all. You don't have to be good for me. I don't need it and can cope without it, but in fact you are good for me' (Guntrip, 1975: 153). The disclosure clearly had a profound effect upon Guntrip: 'Here at last I had a mother who could value her child.' This comment, as I show below, accords with the experience of others who came into contact with him – that Winnicott made them feel special.

The resolution of Guntrip's early trauma, that had been interpreted in complementary ways by each of his two analysts, in fact took place after he had stopped seeing Winnicott. Guntrip became ill through over-work; this was followed by Winnicott having 'flu, from which he died. The night Guntrip heard the news of Winnicott's death he had the first of a series of dreams in which he was eventually able to work through the failure of his mother to relate to him and his brother. Winnicott being one who recognized the significance of ending therapy, it is ironic (in a positive sense) that his death should have provided Guntrip with the means of completing his analytic quest before his own death four years later.

This is another example that confirms Winnicott's conviction that therapy can only assist natural developmental processes: it cannot make them happen before they are ready. (It perhaps also confirms, if death is interpreted as a type of failure, just how significant even his dying was for Guntrip, even if I do not forget that I have already quoted Winnicott's injunction to the analyst to stay alive as long as therapy is ongoing.) Winnicott was himself not over-concerned about symptom relief as the principal outcome of therapy. To have such a view of the aim of analysis would be to extend an early Freudian model of the need for satisfaction and relief to therapy itself. Winnicott, like Fairbairn and Guntrip, favoured the model which Freud began to develop, and which they and others took up more thoroughly, that we are 'object-seeking'. Such a view leads also to a different aim for therapy. To Winnicott this meant, as Guntrip recalled him saying: 'We differ from Freud. He was for curing symptoms. We are concerned with living persons, whole living and loving' (Guntrip, 1975: 153).

Teacher and Supervisor

Since psychotherapy was Winnicott's preoccupation, it is in that sphere of practice that there is the most evidence of his style. There are only glimpses in the literature of him as a teacher and supervisor. In a personal communication quoted by Little one of his students wrote:

> He taught you to free-associate *as an analyst* to all your patient's material. When you had told him about it he would lean back, close his eyes, and begin to talk, chuntering away to himself, apparently associating freely, about the patient, about what you had said, anything that had happened. Not criticising, not asking, 'Why did you say that?' but sharing his associations with you. (Little, 1990: 76)

Another psychotherapist (a young analyst at the time) writes: 'He had the quality of making one feel special. I feel I had a direct line to W., and I'm sure many others did. While bestowing this reassuring feeling to one he somehow always managed to convey that *he* was special – a sort of collusion took place; not a paranoid collusion against a hostile world, but a cosy embrace' (personal communication).

That direct line is also clear from Judith Issroff's description of an *ad hoc* supervision session with Winnicott. Her picture is reminiscent, in a number of ways, of a guru. She had used the squiggle game with one of her young patients, and ended a session with two hundred of them, about which she understood very little. She phoned Winnicott and took the material round to him. He was 'huddled' in a baggy knitted jacket, perched on a pouffe, although he soon ended up on the floor (as was apparently usual in these circumstances),

> sitting close to the ground, elbow on knees, his spectacles pushed way back on his brow . . . his forehead gripped and supported on his hand, peeping between his fingers . . . [He] looked and listened carefully with a somewhat grim expression, silent till I came to the end, the papers scattered round him on the floor. Then he raised his gaze ceilingward and with narrowed eyes, in a rather thin, faint voice, sighed a cryptic, '*We must remember the creativity of salivation.* Good-bye!' And so I departed even more mystified than when I arrived. (Issroff, 1993: 42–3, her italics)

This was not unusual in Issroff's experience of seminars or supervision with Winnicott, although she learned to store away what she had not understood of 'Winnicott's insightful utterances' until a time when she could make use of them.

There are many others, who never knew Winnicott, and who perhaps do not always read him as thoroughly as he deserves, who similarly have stored away 'Winnicott's insightful utterances', unsure precisely what they always mean, but intuitively believing that they are highly relevant to their own practice of therapy and counselling. In his writing (as the reader will have discovered here) he provides a mine of delightful phrases. Some of them have the same enigmatic quality as his response to Issroff, making them, like the messages of ancient oracles capable of different interpretations. It is perhaps this that makes it less tempting (and in fact less easy) to copy him in any set way of working in therapy. Indeed, Winnicott's spontaneity and originality – even if sometimes he appears to contradict himself – should encourage therapists and counsellors alike 'to find their own individual ways of working, not to follow his, because these belonged essentially and inseparably with his personality' (Little, 1990: 76).

This is made more possible because it is neither possible nor desirable to identify a formal 'Winnicottian' school, whether of theory or method. His influence has been considerable, as I show in Chapter 5, although it is seen more in the way certain people have followed through particular ideas, rather than being built upon a comprehensive philosophical system or pragmatic base (as is the case with the followers of several other figures in this series). But before examining the way Winnicott's ideas have been taken up by others, I look in the next chapter at the various criticisms that can be made of his position.

4

Criticisms and Rebuttals

Introduction

Winnicott is essentially a writer for those in the caring professions, although it is rare to find anyone outside psychoanalysis and psychotherapy taking issue with him. His name may have become a by-word in the related field of counselling, but his ideas attract little actual debate (even if some of them become catch-phrases) within that related profession. He has also made little impact on wider intellectual culture. This is in itself an indication that he is not of the stature of Freud, with whom some would compare him. There is not, even within the other major related discipline of psychology, any great degree of interest in his ideas; if behaviourism (represented by, for example, Eysenck) continues to have running battles with psychoanalysis, Winnicott does not attract any specific fire. It is principally in Winnicott's own field of discourse, as this chapter amply demonstrates, that we find appropriate qualification of his theories, criticism of some of his shortcomings, and arguments about some of his basic assumptions. Most commonly there is general appreciation of his work, with particular emphases highlighted as differences from other analytic thinking, and with particular reservations expressed about some parts of his total work.

There may be reasons why there is little major criticism of his whole work. It is possible, for example, that the nature of his writing is such that debate is necessarily quite limited. He may have written prolifically, but he published little that was presented as a comprehensive theory. For instance, *Playing and Reality* (1971a), even if it is laid out as 'a proper book with a developing argument . . . is in fact a compilation of articles written independently of one another but strung together by linking passages to give it some semblance of unity' (Rycroft, 1985: 143). There is no clear schema in Winnicott, with the possible exception of *Human Nature* (1988b); even then it would be unfair to judge his theory as a polished whole from a posthumously published book that was only in draft form at the time of his death (and had been through many revisions since 1954). Rycroft, himself another key figure in the independent psychoanalytic group in Britain, is particularly critical of Winnicott's lack of acknowledgement of his sources or of parallel ideas in others. Despite 'great admiration' for him (1985: 20), he denounces Winnicott's theorizing, 'in spite of the occasional use of abstract nouns', as 'a personal statement, too idiosyncratic to be readily assimilated into the general body of any scientific theory. He often sounds like a voice crying in a wilderness that is in fact inhabited, or like a visionary who is disguising himself as a thinker' (1985: 144).

There is also little even in the way of a more compact theoretical position (except perhaps his theory of the development of the self) that can be debated as readily as, for example, Freud can be on instinct theory, the unconscious, the centrality of sexuality, or the structure of the personality. Winnicott embarked on no grand 'project' as Freud did. There are of course innovative ideas, such as transitional objects and transitional phenomena; and it can be argued that his conception of external reality as being constructed out of destruction in fantasy (1965b: 75-6) and his work on creativity are major contributions and real departures, on a par with Klein's work (Farhi, personal communication). Neither do I forget such innovative techniques as the spatula game; but with such few exceptions there is nothing in Winnicott quite as developed as Klein's concept of 'positions' (Segal, 1992: 33-40) or, for example, as the structure of the personality in Jung's theoretical framework. This is not to dispute that in places he is as bold and as controversial as any.

While his work is often equated with Bowlby's, he did no detailed research as his contemporary did – even if some of Bowlby's methodology might be open to dispute. Furthermore, while it may be difficult to place Winnicott in a particular theor-etical camp, as a Freudian or a Kleinian, it is also impossible (as the next chapter shows) to describe those who come after him as 'Winnicottian'. Not only would that be contrary to his view of himself and his work; it is also a consequence of a creative style which is essentially limited to certain areas of interest. It is more likely that a therapist or counsellor will say, 'I value Winnicott's ideas about transitional objects (or whatever)', than that they will claim, 'I am a Winnicottian'. To be a 'Winnicottian' alone would be to leave considerable gaps in both theory and practice; or would be to claim for Winnicott what belongs more to psychoanalytic thought and practice as a whole.

If I appear critical of him for not presenting a coherent theory, that is not my intention. In itself this is no reason for criticism: people may contribute partially to theory and practice without having to present a whole. I have made it clear already in earlier chapters that he was a creative and original thinker on a grand scale, even if he did not work towards a grand scheme. His writing is undoubtedly full of intended as well as unintended paradox, as Clancier and Kalmanovitch recognize in the title of their book *Winnicott and Paradox* (1987). Some of the inherent contradictions in his writing arise because he constantly developed his ideas and inevitably refined them, as one might expect of any dynamic investigator; but also partly perhaps because he seems to have been as little concerned about his own precedents as he was about those set by other writers who might have influenced him.

Greenberg and Mitchell quote one such paradox: 'the separation that is not a separation but a form of union' (Winnicott, 1971a: 98); and they suggest that Winnicott's very style of presentation reflects the issues he is most concerned with, both in human development and in psychoanalysis itself: how to preserve a central core without becoming isolated (Greenberg and Mitchell, 1983: 190). Indeed Winnicott recognized in that very context that the relationship between originality and tradition is 'one more example, and a very exciting one, of the interplay between separateness and union' (Winnicott, 1971a: 99). Greenberg and Mitchell observe how he 'entices, baffles and provokes his readers, valuing them highly but never confronting them directly' (1983: 190). John Davis, who describes himself as one of those who sat at Winnicott's feet, observes that Winnicott was essentially concerned with exploration, and with telling people what he had found. 'It was not for arguing; it was for taking away and using, if you can' (personal communication). Davis cites the parallel of Sir Alexander Fleming, who discovered penicillin, even if he was also not a good teacher. We should not expect Winnicott to be good at everything.

All this tends to leads to different assessments of him. Some might take him or leave him as a whole; but it is more likely that most will take various ideas from him, and even inspiration from him, particularly from his open-mindedness. Few therapists or counsellors would want to disagree totally with him, because many of his ideas rarely rouse fierce differences of opinion. Those who take to him often do so because of his style, his approach and the attractiveness of his creative expressions. Criticism of Winnicott therefore tends to be of detail, although more often it is the case that the literature that cites him does so because his ideas have provided the incentive for further exploration of fascinating themes.

What this chapter can therefore most usefully do is to indicate the areas of disagreement that have become apparent, mainly in psychoanalytic literature, where quite a number of papers specifically explore how Winnicott's ideas might inform theory and practice. This type of critique is much more evident than any academic analysis of his conceptual framework, methodology and logical argument. My final chapter provides the opportunity to look at other fields where Winnicott has been influential, although it is interesting that there is also little actual critique of him in those fields. In social work and in particular in child care, for example, we typically find the use of his ideas rather than a critical discussion of them; and even in academic psychology, in those centres where there is an interest in him, there is generally more concern to develop some of his concepts so that they can then be studied, rather than to criticize ideas which in themselves are not capable of verification.

There are also some contrasts that can usefully be identified between Winnicott on the one hand and either Freud or Klein on the other, and it is these which I address in the first two sections. It has to be said, however, that Greenberg and Mitchell (1983: 205–9), as I noted in Chapter 2, identify several places where Winnicott misreads Freud, making it difficult sometimes to know whether he was aware of the differences between himself and the earlier tradition which he liked to be seen to espouse.

Optimism and Pessimism

There is a considerable difference between Winnicott's attitude towards persons and that of both Freud and Klein, where a bleak (sometimes in Freud even a disillusioned) view of humanity contrasts with a more optimistic appeal to the positive in Winnicott. Rudnytsky observes that 'Freud's preoccupation with the sense of guilt identifies him as an heir of St Augustine,' whereas 'the playfulness and paradoxicality of Winnicott make him akin rather more to Erasmus' (1989: 345). Winnicott rejects the death instinct, which Freud first posited and which Klein was almost alone amongst his immediate followers in taking up.

It is not that Winnicott fails to assign a place to ruthlessness, envy and greed. His paper on 'The development of the capacity for concern' (1965b: 73-82) discusses guilt and reparation, and the ruthless expression of instinctual drives. The mother is portrayed here very much like Freud's or Klein's libidinal object. At the same time there is a key difference, because Winnicott uses the term 'concern' in preference to the word 'guilt', and suggests that the infant feels protective towards and cares for the 'holding environment' aspect of the mother less from a sense of guilt (as in Klein), but more from a sense of gratitude. 'The infant feels grateful because he can destroy and love the object and the object survives . . . love is alive and strong enough to use destructiveness creatively, rendering guilt superfluous' (Eigen, 1981: 418). Eigen also points out how Klein leaves little room for joy, which she could interpret as a manic defence. Joy ('ego-orgasm') and creativity in Winnicott are not defences but fundamental parts of human experience.

From the Kleinian point of view Winnicott is to be criticized for making the baby too benign, and for idealizing motherhood, which, as I show below, feminists also hold against him. As Segal observes, there is no emphasis in Winnicott on the way the child (or the adult) creates and maintains the splits in the internal world. His lack in this respect deprives the child or the adult of the opportunity to take control of this splitting mechanism. Furthermore, 'Winnicott implies a strong disagreement with all that Klein and her successors have described about the processes of projection, in which the hated and "bad" aspects of the self and the objects/people inside are projected into or seen in people outside' (Segal, 1992: 94–5).

As I recount further below, there is some concern that Winnicott does not describe a sufficiently real ambivalence in human relating. At this point it is worth noting how his recognition of the reality of positive features stands in some contrast to the Freudian and Kleinian tendency to treat the positive with suspicion. Such analysts not only tend to see the positive as a reaction formation against aggression and destructiveness, but also sometimes seem to place the latter rather than the former at the core of the personality.

Illusion

There may be similar disagreements in analytic circles about the concept of illusion. Winnicott is not alone in assigning to it a positive place in human development, but his view is in such contradistinction to Freud's that Winnicott's legitimization of the role of illusion is 'liable to arouse in us the suspicion of irrationalism'; use of the term in this way 'might be suspected of containing residues of infantile neurosis' (Usuelli, 1992: 179, 180).

The philosopher Antony Flew similarly suggests (1978: 492–6) that Winnicott's view of illusion is self-defeating, especially in Winnicott's claim that the beliefs of a sane person are of the same order as those characteristic of people we call mad. Indeed on not a few occasions Winnicott deliberately employs the concept of madness to describe normal developmental processes, such as when he says that primary maternal preoccupation in any other circumstance might be called an illness. In a reply to Flew's criticism Flarsheim observes the distinction that Winnicott draws between illusion and delusion (Flarsheim, 1978: 508), the former more aptly describing the sane person, the latter the mad person. While Flew is happy to follow Winnicott in the Freudian conviction that religious beliefs are illusions (although here he fails to appreciate Winnicott's positive gloss, which is diametrically opposed to Freud's negative interpretation), he is less happy about the suggestion that illusion is inherent in all art. Unfortunately Flew spoils his argument by exploiting for his own rationalist agenda a minor example of Winnicott's about Catholic and Protestant differences on the bread and wine in communion. He also allows little room for the use of metaphor, which may be one way of understanding Winnicott's use of illusion in relation to religion and art, as a third way of understanding that lies between fact and falsity.

Winnicott's view of the significance of illusion finds acceptance elsewhere, for example in the work of Searles. He cites Winnicott and himself comments that 'daily living, even in adulthood, involves continual increments of illusion and disillusion, and, in successful maturation, in increasing "skill" in experiencing illusionment and disillusionment, as one develops an increasingly confident and creative approach to one's environment, and as one's ability to appraise outer and inner reality becomes increasingly accurate' (Searles, 1965: 612–13). Rycroft concedes that the idea of transitional reality 'is perhaps the most important contribution made to psychoanalytic theory in the last thirty years' (1985: 145), but points out that it is not entirely original, quoting a number of poets who have said the same of creative imagination. Imagination is also an important theme for Rycroft (1968).

Freud's view of illusion is that it represents, whether on the level of the universal (such as religion) or the individual, the fulfilment of a strong and early wish. Although he does not equate illusion with an error in thinking (in other words errors are not necessarily illusions), there is a strong sense in his writing that all illusions are examples of erroneous thinking, with the additional factor of being charged emotionally by the desire for wish-fulfilment. Freud gives as an example Columbus' 'discovery' of a new route to the Indies, when he came across what we still know as the West Indies. It was an illusion to think he had discovered the (East) Indies, not just because it was an error, but because Columbus strongly *wished* to find such a route. Throughout Freud's particular essay on this subject (1927) he desires to replace illusion with reality-testing and rational thought. Just as the pleasure principle in individual development needs to be tempered and even replaced by the reality principle, so Freud would wish reason and truth to reign supreme over illusory thinking.

Winnicott transforms the term 'illusion' radically. Not only does illusion become a means by which a child gradually relates to the other and to the external world, but each disillusion which the mother helps the child to experience (beginning with the disillusion about omnipotence) is replaced by a different illusion. The capacity for illusion remains as a positive means of meeting new situations throughout life – a type of transitional space. Indeed, we might go even further and state that what Winnicott suggests is that reality is in fact unknowable, and that we live in a world of shared illusions. The unknowability of ultimate reality, apart from its discussion in philosophy and theology, is of course found elsewhere in psycho-analytic thought, such as in Bion's use of the sign 'O' to denote absolute truth: 'it can be known about, its presence can be recognized and felt, but it cannot be known' (Bion, 1977: 30). The closeness of such language to religious discourse drives home a major difference between views about the limitations of knowledge and of perceptions of reality in Winnicott and others, and Freud's unrelenting attack on religion (for a further exploration of this theme with regard to Lacan as well as Winnicott and Bion, see Eigen, 1981).

In fact there is even in Freud some evidence that Winnicott's view of illusion might find some agreement, especially when the term is contrasted with 'delusion'. Usuelli points out a valuable distinction between the two terms: an illusion tends to be *shared* with others, and can be called into question, whereas a deluded person often wishes to *impose* his or her reality and truth upon others. As Usuelli writes, 'the transitions between delusion, religion and ideology are multiple and the boundaries between them are blurred' (1992: 182). Freud also uses the term 'delusion' of a belief that is so improbable and so incompatible with all that we know about reality (1927: 213). It is perhaps possible that his argument could have been better expressed by distinguishing that type of religion which is a form of delusion from that type which is an illusion. Indeed Freud understands how psychoanalysis itself may be of the same order. The difference, he suggests, between the illusion that might be psychoanalysis and the illusion that is religion is that in the case of psychoanalysis you do not get punished for holding different views (not strictly true, as it turned out!), and your views are open to change (1927: 237).

I dwell a little on Freud's position because in the end we find a similar idea to that which Winnicott puts forward: that illusions can change, as new experiences of 'reality' impinge. What Freud does not go on to recognize is that the new version of 'reality' may in its own way similarly be as much an illusion as the belief that has been given up. Usuelli also observes that when Freud put forward the idea of transference – that is, the client treating the therapist as if the therapist were someone other than the therapist, often a figure from the past – this was assumed to be equally illusory. It is not certain whether Freud understands the transference in this way, although as I indicate below he clearly recognizes its transitional quality. The therapeutic relationship has an 'as if' quality to it; and it is to some extent a shared illusion in which the therapist also participates (through the therapist's counter-transference as well as through accepting the transference), in a search for understanding, insight and change. Therapy provides its own transitional space and illusions, which are not immediately taken apart and destroyed, even if they will eventually have to be given up (Usuelli, 1992: 180).

The Transitional Object

Flew comments on the 'extraordinary disproportion' of interest in Winnicott's work on transitional objects and transitional phenomena, given the small amount he said about them relative to his total output (Flew, 1978: 485). It is perhaps, in the apt title of Brody's critique (1980), an 'idealized phenomenon'.

Brody expresses some frustration that Winnicott did not describe the actual observations which led him to posit the idea of the transitional object. She questions whether attachment to the transitional object is as universal as he makes out, referring to research which shows that children brought up in rural areas, where they have much more physical contact with mothers, show much lower frequency of the use of transitional objects. Other findings have suggested that the infants who use transitional objects are weaned earlier, have mothers with less prior experience of babies, and are played with more intensively by their fathers – Brody's review of the literature on transitional objects and phenomena is invaluable here (1980: 595–9). It appears that transitional objects may be more in evidence as substitutes for a missing or distant mother, and therefore more like a comforter than Winnicott is prepared to admit. Brody suggests, for example, that the cloth material that forms part of an infant's bedding may well be perceived as an extension of the infant and must therefore 'be held by him and with him, and . . . must go wherever he goes, so that even a temporary loss of it arouses distress, sometimes panic' (1980: 581).

It is re-assuring to realize that not all children have transitional objects – that indeed is what some mothers say on learning about Winnicott's idea. They even suggest, as I have heard in teaching this topic, that they felt that they themselves must have been the transitional object, since their child did not appear to have one. If the transitional object is a substitute for mother then this makes sense. Furthermore the transitional object is not always as transitional as it seems. Winnicott suggests that the transitional object is gradually given up, and that 'in health the transitional object does not "go inside" nor does the feeling about it necessarily undergo repression' (1975: 233). Perhaps the key phrase here is 'in health'; because a number of investigations show that transitional objects are not necessarily given up but become regressive phenomena. Other symptoms or rituals are developed as the transitional objects are given up.

Brody sums up the current findings about transitional objects and transitional phenomena at the time of writing her article. There is lack of agreement about their universality, since they are more prevalent in families of upper and upper-middle socio-economic status. The degree of attachment to them seems inversely related to maternal nurturing. The mother's approval or disapproval of such an object also seems a key factor – it is therefore questionable how much the infant 'creates' this experience. The object serves oral and tactile gratification, is taken up at between five and twelve months, and unless relinquished by the third year at the latest can scarcely be called transitional. There is no evidence of any relationship between possession of such an object in childhood and sound object relations in childhood or later, or creativity in adult life. In fact many of the statements about transitional objects and transitional phenomena are conjectural. For example, Winnicott suggests a symbolic use of the object, which is too advanced for the mentation of infants, as other research upon their thinking suggests: 'the immaturity of an infant's neuronal development precludes a capacity for symbolic thought' (Brody, 1980: 571). Brody concludes:

> These toys may be called transitional in the sense that they help the child to bridge the time from night to morning, or to bridge the space from one place to another, without feeling too alone or too nostalgic; but they are not the kind of transitional objects meant by Winnicott to represent something between oral erotism and true object relations, unless one refers clearly to delayed, arrested, or regressive behavior with the toy. (1980: 593)

Stern distinguishes between Winnicott's transitional object and 'a personified thing' – a toy or an object which mother uses in play with her baby, and which then becomes used by the baby in the task of integration. The latter is short-lived, appears earlier, engages memory rather than symbolic thinking, and does not imply regression towards self/other differentiation (Stern, 1985: 122–3). Stern also suggests that the child's first words can become 'a personified thing', although he obviously finds Winnicott's ideas in this whole area helpful, and provides some evidence that a child's language (in talking to herself) may be, as Winnicott suggested (1975: 232) a transitional phenomenon (Stern, 1985: 172–3).

Differentiation

Central to Winnicott's writing is the relationship of mother and baby, and central to some of the criticism of him is his emphasis (as well as the effects of this emphasis) on the unitive experience of the nursing couple. Although not critical of the whole of Winnicott's theory, the research described by Daniel Stern gives rise to definite questioning of the earliest undifferentiated stage as it appears in both Winnicott and Mahler (for the latter see for example Mahler et al., 1975): 'In contrast to these views, the present account [Stern's] has stressed the very early formation of a sense of a core self and core other during the life period that other theories allot to prolonged self/other undifferentiation' (Stern, 1985: 101).

The idea of a period of undifferentiation, suggests Stern, even if 'very problematic . . . at the same time . . . has great appeal'. It supposes that once upon a time there was such 'an actual psychobiological wellspring from which such feelings originate and to which one could possibly return' (Stern, 1985: 240). In the end, however, it is a belief rather than a proven state, a belief about 'connectedness, affiliation, attachment and security' (1985: 24). Attachment theory makes connectedness an end point, not a starting point. Stern's theory is that this core-relatedness is to be achieved in the period from two to seven months of age, and that it is the feelings then that 'serve as an emotional reservoir of human connectedness' (1985: 241). Winnicott pushes the symbiotic phase to the earliest point, although in him separateness and relatedness are equal developmental lines. Thus Winnicott differs from Mahler, as he himself made clear, since he rejects the term 'symbiosis' that Mahler uses, as 'too well rooted in biology to be acceptable' (1971a: 130). He even hints at an alternative view to undifferentiation in the following sentence: 'From the observer's point of view there may seem to be object-relating in the primary merged state, but it has to be remembered that at the beginning the object is a "subjective object"' (1971a: 130). Stern's work suggests that the observer may in fact be right.

The Idealization of Mothering

Winnicott's strength lies in his observations of and about mothers and their infants. But strength can also carry implicit weaknesses, and there is now growing criticism of the role he assigns to the mother, making her carry the main share of the care of the baby. She therefore appears to become the one who is solely responsible for the development of her child, for good or ill. Winnicott does not of course blame the mother: if anything he is more critical of doctors and nurses for not permitting the mother to follow her natural intuitive feelings about the care of her child (for example 1988a: 69–81; 1988b: 104). Yet, as Parker observes, he also suggests that the capacity to mother is outside a woman's control – that mothering appears to be something that they either can or cannot do. 'There is room for all kinds of mothers in the world, and some will be good at one thing and some good at another. Or shall I say some will be bad at one thing and some bad at another?' (1988a: 18). At the same time mothers, who in one sense cannot help how they are with their babies, are also 'responsible for the orchestration of a highly complex developmental sequence from an initial sustaining of the infant's omnipotence to organising a graduated failure of adaptation to its demands' (Parker, 1994: 6).

It is, I imagine, difficult to write anything in the field of relationships which does not in one way or another arouse anxieties. There is a sense about Winnicott's task, as much as there is about the mothers he describes, that he and they will be 'damned if you do, damned if you don't'. Segal observes that his emphasis was a necessary counterweight to the Truby King philosophy of the 1930s and 1940s in which, for example, mothers were told to resist their natural inclinations to pick up children when they cried. Yet Segal goes on to say that by his idealization of mothers and their situation, 'Winnicott becomes quite persecuting to real mothers, who find no recognition of their "badness or discomfort"' (Segal, 1992: 95). This is not quite true, because as I showed in Chapter 2, in at least one paper he puts considerable emphasis on a mother's hate (1975: 194–203). He also qualifies the apparent idealization of motherhood – which is seen in the sentiment that 'the good mother knows naturally how to mother if she will only follow her instincts' (Chodorow, 1989: 90) – by the qualification of the phrase 'good-enough mother'. Such a phrase is a relief to some women, but not unnaturally raises in others the question of just what constitutes 'good-enough'.

It is fascinating too just how much the phrase 'good-enough' is used by therapists and counsellors, not just of mothering, but also of their own work: in some way it relieves their anxiety about themselves and their work, to seize on the implied permission to be a 'good-enough' therapist, although the way the term is used sometimes by them makes one wonder whether it has now become a catch-all phrase. Furthermore, use of the phrase runs the risk of masking rather than resolving anxiety about one person's felt or actual responsibility for the welfare of another. It may be a re-assuring term, but there is a danger that its use fails to deal with the real conflicts and ambivalence involved in the therapeutic as well as the maternal role. Like the transitional object, Winnicott's 'good-enough' has become exaggerated in its significance.

A perfect mother, as the feminist analyst Chodorow observes, is 'an infantile fantasy' (1989: 90). Winnicott of course paints a much more comprehensive picture of a mother's ambivalence: I have observed already that the description of the ways in which a mother may hate her baby makes for a more rounded picture (Winnicott, 1975: 194–203). (Ambivalence in psychoanalysis means the presence of intense yet quite contradictory feelings, not wishy-washy 'mixed feelings'.) Yet even here his use of the word 'hate' does not seem altogether appropriate to describe what may well be perfectly normal feelings, for example of relief rather than aggression: a mother can feel overjoyed that someone else can respond to her baby on occasion better than she can herself, when she is tired and wants a break. Such ordinary feelings, of not having to care, or of the pleasure of being able to look after oneself, do not get a mention. The wish to preserve herself against her baby's constant demands need not be hate in the mother. While it is therefore a relief that Winnicott recognizes the normality of violent thoughts towards an infant, the normality of taking pleasure in being able to have time and space for oneself, even in those very early weeks, is obscured. Parker also observes how Winnicott fails to recognize that a mother's hate (or for that matter a father's) is not always contained, but can be acted out 'in ways that range from the surreptitious shake to major abuse' (Parker, 1994: 7).

Parker argues that although Winnicott introduces the concept of ambivalence, his thinking in this area needs more elaboration. Like other critics of this aspect of his theory, she suggests that he (in common with many other analysts) was constrained by his own discipline, which tends to look at life 'from the point of view of the child to the detriment of our understanding of maternal develop-ment' (Parker, 1994: 3). King, whose ironically titled paper 'There Is No Such Thing as a Mother' turns Winnicott's famous phrase neatly upon its head, similarly criticizes his work because, despite it 'being very much focused on mothering, it is rather little concerned with mothers themselves' (1994: 18). In support of this criticism she quotes Winnicott: 'the care of a new-born infant is a whole-time job and . . . can be done well by only one person' (King, 1994: 21).

Chodorow (1978) quotes Winnicott with approval in his warning against the idea of mothering as a 'maternal instinct' (the changes that may take place in a pregnant mother being psychological not instinctual), as well as his phrase 'there is no such thing as a baby', and the concept of a true and false self. She nevertheless criticizes analysts generally and Winnicott particularly (in that she names him with some frequency). Her concern is that 'they do not consider their prescriptions difficult for most "normal" mothers to fulfill' (1978: 85). She cites as an example Winnicott's 'effusive' phrase about mothering being an 'extraordinary condition which is almost like an illness, though it is very much a sign of health' (Chodorow, 1978: 65; Winnicott 1965a: 15). In her critique she goes on to take analysts to task for the stresses they put on the maternal role, its fulfilment and gratification, and on the mutuality and oneness of the mother with the infant. While Chodorow agrees that 'many mothers and infants are mutually gratified through their relationship, and many others enjoy taking care of their infants' (1978: 86), she adds the important qualification that the relationship is experienced differently from the child's and the mother's point of view. The child either relates to the mother or does not relate at all. But the 'mother also participates in her family and in the rest of the community and society' (1978: 86).

Analysts also fail to recognize other features of a woman's position, such as her dependence at that time financially upon her husband, gender roles in child care, etc., about which Chodorow believes sociologists inform us better. Although women analysts 'at least mention a potential psychological asymmetry in the mother–infant mutuality', and stress its value for the infant's development, 'male therapists (Bowlby and Winnicott are cases in point) ignore the mother's involvement outside of her relationship to her infant and her possible interest in mitigating its intensity' (1978: 87). She also criticizes Winnicott for failing to address gender issues. She cites the contradiction in psychoanalytic descriptions that, while all people have the basis of being parents in themselves because they have experienced being parented, only women 'continue to provide parental (we call it "maternal") care. What happens to the potential parenting capacities in males?' (1978: 88).

Fathers

Contemporary psychoanalysis, which as Mancia observes is 'very much indebted to Klein and Winnicott' (1993: 941), focuses on the early stages of development, and emphasizes the maternal figure in parent–child relationships. This overshadows the role of the father, and the importance of the Oedipus complex as it was developed by Freud. Other analysts oppose such an emphasis and still consider regression to the Oedipal situation as more significant in their understanding of psychopathology than disturbances in the mother–child relationship.

I have observed in Chapter 2 that Winnicott assigns a somewhat traditional role to the father, that of supporting the mother, even if he extends this a little by presenting an image of the father facilitating an environment for the mother, which will in turn permit her to provide the right adaptive environment for her baby. His position on fatherhood is that of an orthodox Freudian: the father needs to be there at the beginning of a child's life as sup-portive of mother. Later father provides the example of a separate person, which develops into the role he plays in the Oedipus complex.

Not surprisingly Winnicott comes in for criticism on two counts. The first is that such a scheme assumes that women are the providers and carers in the nuclear family. Thomas (in Ferguson et al., 1993) puts forward the view that such assumptions have been 'bolstered and given credibility by child care experts such as Bowlby and Winnicott' (Ferguson et al., 1993: 184). As already quoted above, Winnicott writes that the care of a new born infant 'can be done well by only one person' (Winnicott, 1964: 24). Winnicott in places shows how the father can assume the role of the mother (1965a: 72–3), but the man is essentially (as he indeed writes) a 'mother-substitute' and not in the role of father. This is also a significant difference from Kleinian theory, where the father protects the child from the mother and the mother from the child, not simply the mother and child from the external world. Segal reminds us that 'Klein believed that the father's support and help is felt by the child to be crucial in restoring the health, goodness, happiness and babies of the mother after the child's phantasied attacks on her' (1992: 95).

Rycroft, reviewing *Playing and Reality*, is similarly critical of Winnicott's lack of feeling for the paternal-masculine. There are only three references to 'father' in the book. Rycroft observes that 'not only do fathers play with children (as opposed to infants) as much as if not more than mothers do, but our culture, in spite of the emancipation of women during this century, still shows obvious traces of being predominantly created and transmitted by men' (1985: 142). This cannot be ignored, as Samuels also points out: he observes that Winnicott (as well as Lacan and Jung, amongst others) fails to acknowledge 'the cultural construction of the father relation' (Samuels, 1993: 147).

Similarly, as noted already in relation to mothering, the relationship of the mother with the father deeply affects the mother–infant relationship – the dyadic mother–child relationship is not one that takes place in isolation. Where the father is viewed on the one hand 'as a present, collaborative, caring object, capable of love, or as a physically and emotionally absent object, or as a sadistic, unreliable and irresponsible one towards the new mother–infant couple' (Mancia, 1993: 942), it would be utterly astonishing if this had no effect. Winnicott never explores any of these possibilities, but only presents the value of the supportive relationship. Mancia's argument, that the more comprehensive view of the way in which the maternal role 'will be deeply affected by the father and his actual affects' (1993: 942), provides yet a third way to understand pathology – not just the father position at the Oedipal stage, nor the mother–infant relationship alone, but 'how important the father can be in the pre-oedipal stages and in the definition of the maternal role in the primary relation' (1993: 942). Following this indirect role the father then plays a central part in the triangular relationship, acting as 'an important bulwark against the incestuous wishes of the child' (1993: 944). Mancia also looks at the significance for development of the absent father.

The later period of development is of less interest to Winnicott in his writing, although of course in his clinical work he saw children of all ages, as well as adults, and naturally worked with the significance of the father relationship in many cases. In Chapter 3 I have already cited Winnicott's case of Alfred, and the effect on the boy of his father's hospitalization. In his paper on the effect of psychotic parents, Winnicott certainly recognizes illness in the father as of significance in later childhood. Nevertheless even in that context he has a tendency to emphasize the positive and neglect the possible consequences of the negative, providing an example of a boy he first saw at the age of eleven in an acute psychotic episode. His father was schizophrenic, his mother schizoid, yet Winnicott suggests that both parents saw the boy through his illness, and 'thanks very largely to his very ill parents, he is now healthy' (1965a: 76–7).

Winnicott's idea of the father's access to the baby via the mother is also contradicted by research, as Samuels points out, citing Hopkins (1990). Samuels further illustrates the insignificance of the father in Winnicott by quoting the statement from one paper in *The Family and Individual Development* that father's illness does not 'impinge on a child's life in earliest infancy . . . first the infant must be old enough to recognize the father as a man' (1965a: 73). Samuels sets out his own idea of *paternal* holding, as parallel to but different from Winnicott's *maternal* holding (Samuels, 1993: 158), since in Samuels' view holding includes erotic and aggressive feed-back; and in his desire to be inclusive, this becomes a metaphorical concept that transcends the actual gender of parent and child. In the end Samuels brings us no closer to the distinctiveness of the paternal role, even though he restores its importance to a position which resembles Freud's earlier recognition of the vital place of the father in the anal and Oedipal stages.

In his understanding of the child of two years onwards Winnicott certainly tends to be conventional in his views, and this affects his view of the place of the father in the child's experience. By way of reply we might say that his real strength lay in his observation and work on the mother–baby relationship in the first six months of life. As far as he was concerned, that was the crucial time: 'Give me a child for four devoted months,' Professor Davis recalls Winnicott saying, 'and you cannot disturb its self-confidence' (personal com-munication). If that appears to over-emphasize the role of the mother, then perhaps any specialist can be criticized for concen-trating upon one area alone. Nevertheless, enough has been said here to show that Winnicott's one-sided emphasis on the mother is a serious weakness.

Gender Differences

In Chodorow's famous study of mothering she devotes considerable attention to examining gender differences in the pre-Oedipal period. Winnicott at this point drops out of her picture, since it is a subject upon which he wrote extremely little, and an area upon which he is generally weak. There is a hint of gender awareness in 'Hate in the Counter-Transference' (1975: 201), where Winnicott writes about 'reasons why a mother hates her baby, even a boy' (as if, it might be noted, a girl could be hated more easily). Perhaps even here he only uses the phrase because Freud, quoted by Winnicott in the sentence before, refers to a mother's love for the baby boy. The closest he gets to an examination of gender issues is in his papers on the origins of creativity (1971a: 72–85) and on feminism (1986: 193–4), where Winnicott differentiates between the female and the male elements in both genders. The interest in his case example in *Playing and Reality* (1971a: 72–9) is less for anything original about gender, more for his creative interventions: for example, 'I know perfectly well that you are a man but I am listening to a girl . . . It is *I* who see the girl and hear the girl talking, when actually there is a man on my couch. The mad person is *myself* ' (1971a: 73).

Winnicott uses the familiar distinction of 'being' and 'doing' about gender differences – although it is worth remembering that Freud had already dismissed such attempts to identify male and female as the equivalents of 'active' and 'passive' by confining these adjectives to the ovum and the sperm in reproduction. Although not quite consistent when it comes to moral thinking, Freud sees all other psychological distinctions between male and female as social constructions. Rycroft is rightly critical of Winnicott's categorization of 'calm' as 'feminine', and 'desire' (even female desire) as 'masculine', which 'reads strangely when one remembers that nowadays even ladies move' (Rycroft, 1985: 142); although to be fair to Winnicott Rycroft seems to have omitted reading the footnote where Winnicott states that '"active" and "passive" are not correct terms, and I must continue the argument using the terms that are available' (1971a: 76n).

Neither is it altogether fair to highlight Winnicott's lack of engagement with these issues. Like many of his psychoanalytic generation he accepted the 'predisposition toward bisexuality' (1971a: 72), but did not explore these issues. Even his 'This Feminism' paper on gender differences has little to say about society itself and what we now recognize as crucial political structures.

The Significance of Societal Structures

We have to remember that the feminist critique of psychoanalysis, typified by Chodorow, of the way motherhood is regarded by a male-dominated society and profession, does not single out Winnicott in particular, even if he is in some ways a good candidate for such criticism, with his particular (male) focus on the mother–infant relationship. It can be argued that, as is the case with Freud, he is the typical product of a patriarchal society, and that the feminist analysis of political structures came too late to influence his work.

Samuels, writing on object relations theory and political change, suggests that there has been a consensus between the Kleinians and the Winnicottians (Samuels actually employs this adjective) that has led to a tendency 'to rule out sociopolitical or other collective aspects of psychological suffering' (Samuels, 1993: 275). His criticism is of object relations theory generally, not of Winnicott in particular, although, as I have observed above, Samuels identifies him by name in his criticism of the way he fails to understand the role of the father in political structures, as well as in the family.

In another chapter Samuels quotes Winnicott's letter to Mrs Chamberlain about combating anti-Semitism (Samuels, 1993: 296), and this is a reminder that Winnicott actually had a strong commitment to political concerns. This is also reflected in some of his published correspondence as well as in various occasional papers that address societal issues. He delivered papers on democracy and on the monarchy, as well as the somewhat condescendingly titled 'This Feminism' (1986: 183–94). In *Home is Where We Start From* the editors title the nine papers in Part 3 'Reflections on Society' (1986). The paper on feminism, delivered in 1963, was in many ways ahead of its time and shows his concern for the topic. The opening words are: 'This is the most dangerous thing I have done in recent years' (1986: 183). But generally the paper is a disappointment and reveals a one-sided realization of the feminist argument. Only once does he refer to the sociological dimension, to describe the mass delusion in men that makes them 'emphasize the "castrated" aspect of the female personality' (1986: 187). He suggests here that male envy of women is greater than female envy of men. Otherwise the paper is more about gender differences and male–female relationships than about the sociological or political perspective. There is more recognition in his essay on democracy (1986: 239–59) of the powerful place of the mother in the life of every infant (as the feminist writer Dinnerstein (1987) similarly argues). This makes 'fear of WOMAN . . . a powerful agent in society structure, and . . . responsible for the fact that in very few societies does a woman hold the political reins' (Winnicott, 1986: 252). What Winnicott does not appear to acknowledge is the reverse direction of this relationship, how societal pressures and structures impinge upon the mother–baby dyad and upon family life. Although 'impingement' is an important concept for him (the mother allows the external world gradually to impinge upon her infant), the external world for Winnicott's nursing couple is generally the immediate environment, and not the wider world as it affects the maternal function.

Sexuality

It has been suggested that Winnicott neglected infantile sexuality. It is indeed the case that 'sexuality is not named or it is so in a very restrictive way' (Clancier and Kalmanovitch, 1987: 124). André Green observes that there is in Winnicott what Green calls a 'forgetting', in the sense of a distraction from the sexual. If he speaks about sexuality it is by not naming it, but naming instead what Green highlights as the 'anti-sexual' factors – what is not

there for some patients is more important than the things that are
(Clancier and Kalmanovitch, 1987: 125). The Oedipus complex
itself features little, except as an accepted Freudian concept with
which he has no quarrel – but then it does not appear at all in
Bowlby's three volumes on *Attachment and Loss*. Perhaps in one
respect this is to be expected, since Winnicott's interest lies with the
nursing couple, rather than three-person relationships. Nevertheless
Greenberg and Mitchell quote one passage where Winnicott's
description of the Oedipus complex (Winnicott, 1965b: 16–17),
which he links with Freud, is in fact a modified description,
drawing upon Klein, without apparently realizing it. Certainly he
does refer to her work. Greenberg and Mitchell observe that 'Klein
explicitly addressed the differences between her account of the
oedipal crisis and Freud's. Winnicott does not: he rewrites Freudian
theory through a Kleinian perspective, preserving an illusion of
consensus and unbroken tradition' (1983: 207). In one paper
Winnicott makes much of his male patient's penis envy as an
indication of the 'girl' Winnicott sees in the patient, without any
recognition there of the likelihood of penis envy being as much a
feature in a man's mind as in a woman's (1971a: 73), despite his
earlier paper on feminism – referred to above – including that
possibility. He explores the significance in this patient of the way
his mother saw him as a girl, but does not go any further into what
are today recognized as crucial issues of socialization and
identification in gender and sexual roles.

Clancier and Kalmanovitch point out that a more careful reading
of Winnicott, particularly the work described in *Holding and
Interpretation* (Winnicott, 1989a), makes it clear that he referred to
and worked towards the resolution of the Oedipus complex when
working with patients who had reached that point in their
development (Clancier and Kalmanovitch, 1987: 95–7). At the
same time we have to remember that other innovative analysts,
such as Klein and Lacan, re-interpreted the Oedipus complex and
detected its significance even in the early mother–baby relationship.
In this part of psychoanalytic theory Winnicott is surprisingly
conventional.

A Philosophical Critique

Grolnick et al. in their edited volume of appreciation of Winnicott's
work, thoughtfully invited the British philosopher Antony Flew to
comment upon the transitional object, since Winnicott's observations have 'obvious philosophical implications' (Flew, 1978:
483). I have already referred to Flew's criticism both of this concept

and of illusion. Some of his other observations apply to most analysts as much as to Winnicott. He attacks, for example, 'untidy theoretical propositions, adultomorphic conceptions, and over-generalization' (1978: 483). Flew comments that Winnicott's concepts seem to belong to a world of flux (1978: 491), but even if the concepts are themselves tidied up, as Flew tries to do, Winnicott makes mistakes that are typical of much psychoanalytic thought. Generalizations are made from specific instances, to make them appear that they cover 'all mankind in every place and period' (1978: 491).

Flew agrees that transitional objects, as defined by Winnicott in his paper on them (Winnicott, 1975: 229), deserve study, although he clearly thinks that these notions, if useful, are also limited. 'The trouble comes when – before you have even started to get to grips with whatever falls within the scope of that original limited notion – you proceed so enormously to extend in one way or another its range of application that of its original meaning only probably the now unwarranted overtones remain' (Flew, 1978: 491). Transitional objects are observably important to children, yet the question needs to be asked whether they have a continuing influence on adult life. Flew identifies some contradictions in the paper, where, for example, Winnicott (as I observed in Chapter 2) describes as his first clinical example a toy rabbit which he proceeds to call a comforter, not a true transitional object. Winnicott also suggests that the loss of a true transitional object would be more important than loss of the mother (1975: 235). Flew rightly finds it hard to believe that loss of a transitional teddy bear would really be greater than that of mother. In his reply to Flew, Flarsheim agrees with Flew's literal understanding of the sentence, but suggests that 'what Winnicott intended was that the transitional object is experienced by the child as more important than the mother when the relationship with the mother is intact and so secure that it can be taken for granted' (Flarsheim, 1978: 507). The reply does not make sense, since it is a non-intact relationship with the mother that is the substance of the original comparison.

Flew accepts, even if it is not possible to say that a baby creates the transitional object as such, that what the baby does is to employ an object (which someone else has created and made available) in a particular way. It is therefore 'the use of the object' that is more important than the object itself. This phrase 'the use of an object' is of course one of Winnicott's own, as Flew acknowledges (Winnicott, 1971a: xi–xii and 86–94). Flew is also critical of Winnicott for being reluctant to give examples of transitional phenomena, because they are so different (1971a: xii). Winnicott's reason is not sufficient, especially when he then goes on to use a phrase such as 'by this definition'. His reluctance to give examples means there has been *no* definition. Flew's third question is what the transitions are between. He is sceptical of transitional phenomena being an intermediate area of experience, a type of third world between external reality and the internal world. The important philosophical principle of Ockham's razor suggests that we should not posit any new worlds that are not necessary. Why, asks Flew, should we have to say that the experience belongs to a third world? Why can it not belong to the second of the original two – psychic reality? (Flew, 1978: 498). Flarsheim's reply to Flew is that the area of illusion is not in fact a third world, but an integration of two worlds, 'external perception on the one hand and dream and hallucination on the other' (Flarsheim, 1978: 509). The problem is exacerbated because Winnicott uses the terms 'space' and 'zone' to describe this third type of experience, suggesting thereby a separate world.

In the end Flew wonders whether he has a 'deeply motivated psychic blindness which inhibits me from joining the chorus of welcome' (1978: 499) for Winnicott's concept. Flarsheim's response to the critique does not venture to reply to that question. He does suggest, however, that what the clinician recognizes, which the philosopher perhaps does not, is the similarity between the concept of the transitional area, and transference reactions in therapy, because 'the patient finds himself feeling and reacting toward the therapist as though the therapist were some figure out of the patient's past, while remaining all the time aware of the present reality of his own identity, the identity of the therapist, and the realities of the treatment situation' (Flarsheim, 1978: 509). Freud anticipated this when he wrote that 'transference . . . creates an intermediate region between illness and real life through which transition from one to the other is made' (1914: 154).

The Therapeutic Relationship

Peter Lomas, himself an innovative writer, who is more openly critical of traditional psychoanalytic technique than Winnicott, acknowledges that Winnicott's is 'perhaps the most important contribution to our understanding of the phenomenon of therapeutic breakdown' (Lomas, 1987a: 83). Nevertheless he draws out certain areas where either lack of clarity or a narrow use of terminology weakens Winnicott's position. For example, Lomas suggests there is lack of clarity in using the same terminology for the whole process of breakdown and the more 'immediate, transient dramatic happenings in a particular session' (1987a: 86). Regression is also more ambiguous than Winnicott suggests: 'it can be powerfully destructive' as well as creative, the latter being Winnicott's almost sole position. The value of Winnicott's ideas is also compromised by his idealization of the holding and protective function of therapy. Not only does he sometimes present it 'as requiring an almost superhuman sensitivity, patience and tolerance' (1987a: 87), but he also tends to interpret the security of holding in phrases which are 'comfortable illusions and denials' (1987a: 90). Support surely needs to be given to clients, but according to each client's needs, with room for challenge as well as comfort. Winnicott, Lomas believes, tends to over-dramatize, and it may well be that his charisma masks an over-simplification of the ideal mother.

Similarly, while Lomas acknowledges that Winnicott's work has encouraged therapists to adopt a more relaxed attitude in general, he comments upon how much Winnicott concentrates on the needs of the client, to the apparent exclusion of the therapist's needs. Spontaneity in therapy appears to be confined to reactions to the unconscious needs of the client, and becomes a special therapeutic response. Lomas would prefer that spontaneity should also include the therapist's feelings about his or her own needs, so that 'the hazards of ordinary life are admitted into the consulting room' (1987a: 93), including the emotions of the therapist.

Winnicott defended himself against critics more orthodox than Lomas, who said that his approach to treatment encouraged both too much regression and too much gratification of infantile wishes, by arguing that regression to dependence is 'organized'; and that meeting the needs of primary narcissism enables the true self to start 'anew . . . to meet environmental failure situations without organization of the defences that involve a false self protecting the true self' (1975: 286).

Conclusion

Although it is possible to find qualifications in Winnicott's extensive canon of writing that counter some of the criticisms of his ideas made in this chapter, there is a danger in using his work as such an arsenal. It is worth remembering that Winnicott was himself not good at dealing with criticism. The New York reception for his paper 'The Use of an Object' (1971a: 86–94), to which I referred in Chapter 1, is one example of his reaction, where he whimsically suggested he tear his paper to pieces – surely an extreme measure, with a hint that 'if you do not like all of this, then I will remove it all'. Another source has suggested to me independently that Winnicott could become incoherent at a meeting if he was subjected to too much criticism; and, according to yet another, he 'used to get quite angry, and try to get the sympathy of the audience on his side in a slightly manipulative way' (personal communications).

I do not cite such opinions to plead for carefulness in questioning his ideas. These observations may suggest, however, the type of thinker and writer that Winnicott was and was not. He was someone who loved to share his creative ideas, and enjoyed the audience's response when, as must normally have been the case outside his own particular professional circles, it was favourable. He was invited to many societies and meetings, and was obviously a popular speaker. He had a rougher ride at his own professional society's 'scientific meetings'.

But he was not, in a strict sense, either of an academic or of a scientific bent, even though his writing clearly merits and receives academic scrutiny, and even if he liked to see himself in the tradition of Darwin and Freud. The imprecision of his terms, his failure to see contradictions (or his belief that contradictions were a form of paradox, and that the use of paradox was sufficient explanation), and his playing with ideas as they came: all these make for a particular style which is hard to define – part poetry, part inventive, part philosophical, and at the same time never setting out to be any one of these types of discourse.

That his name appears so often – sometimes (as this chapter shows) in critical attention to his work, sometimes and more frequently (as the next chapter shows) as an inspiration for the developing work of others – means that Winnicott's ideas are inevitably and necessarily going to be examined with care. Those who are able to conduct quantifiable research are in a position to see how much of what he writes is verifiable. Those whose interest lies in the world of ideas can pursue the internal logic of psychoanalytic discourse. Those who seek to apply his ideas to practice might test out how transferable they are to their own situations. All such attempts demonstrate the catalytic effect Winnicott has on theory and practice. There can be little doubt that he would have enjoyed being in this position, although he might not have been so well equipped to deal with the detailed attention that has been and will continue to be given to his work. There is little doubt either, as is reflected in the final chapter, that – despite the criticisms – his ideas, his poetic touch, his philosophical musings and his unorthodox therapeutic manner exercise considerable fascination for many therapists and counsellors, as well as other professionals.

5

The Overall Influence of D. W. Winnicott

Despite the temptation by some of those who write about Winnicott to elevate his status to a pioneer in his own generation of the same stature as Freud was in his, the last chapter in itself demonstrates how Winnicott's influence is in fact much more limited, since it is in psychoanalytic discourse that the criticisms of him have principally appeared. Outside that discipline Winnicott does not evoke anything like the same level of interest that Freud does: the level of criticism, however negative it may sometimes be, is a sure indication of the significance of a particular writer. Freud's ideas continue to provoke debate; and if his theories have triggered an explosion of interest in a variety of disciplines, it is because he has opened up areas of universal concern.

The last chapter also shows that the psychoanalytic world has not idolized Winnicott. Analysts are often searching critics, of their own number as well as of other therapies. Nevertheless, I began this book with the observation that in many quarters, by which I meant the rather wider world of counselling and psychotherapy, Winnicott remains a firm favourite as a model for the practitioner, and as a creative observer and thinker. That many of his phrases, even if at times they represent only a taste of his ideas, have become so memorable is an indication of the extent of his influence in that particular world. There he is perhaps the most cited of all the second and third generation of analysts.

This is not of course in itself a sign of lasting or deeper influence: Winnicott's disarming phrases can be used as slogans, lacking any real substance. That he should be followed slavishly appears to have been far from his own wishes – and indeed I have made it clear already that he is not the sort of writer who sets out a systematic theory that is comprehensive enough to form the basis for a 'school'. Even if it appears, from some sources at least, that there might have been a part of him that played to the gallery and enjoyed the attention of what was in fact a relatively small circle of 'disciples', there can be no doubt that his addresses and talks to the wider public, his papers at the British Psycho-Analytical Society's meetings, and his informal seminars were opportunities for the generation of ideas that could be floated and discussed. They were, however, never written in stone. Davis and Wallbridge conclude their study of Winnicott's work with these words:

> There is no doubt that we owe much to thinkers in the round – to those who have had the courage to expose themselves, to risk the I AM of setting out for us a whole way of looking at the world, without tacking or trimming, and in spite of those self-doubts which are inevitable in the integrated person and in the person of integrity. To this achievement Winnicott has added a generosity of spirit not always found in the writers on human nature. He has not said to us, 'I am telling you how the world is, so you must think what I think.' He is rather saying, 'On the basis of what we share, and on the basis of how we differ, I may be of use in your own creation of the world.' He wanted to be 'created into and with', to be 'found and used'. He hated the idea of being imitated. (1981: 172)

Compared then to Freud, and perhaps even to Klein or Jung, Winnicott's influence is much more limited, confined (although the list is wide enough!) to particular areas of psychotherapy, psychology, education, social work and other forms of care. As this chapter shows, Winnicott is perhaps most influential as an inspiration to other pioneers, especially those working with children. His energies in life were directed in different professional directions, including support and encouragement of particular forms of care. Since his death his ideas about therapeutic practice and his theories, as they throw light on various developmental issues, have aroused even greater interest than when he was alive, in psychoanalytic circles throughout the world, as well as in a number of other caring professions. There is amongst those who pursue Winnicott's ideas active discouragement for the use of the term 'Winnicottian', because such a term, they claim, is alien to his spirit. There is nonetheless sufficient evidence that Winnicott continues to inform and perhaps influence contemporary thinking in some of the caring professions, as well as considerable evidence to demonstrate how his work has furthered the development of psychodynamic thinking.

The Winnicott Research Unit

Preceding chapters have shown the fascination of Winnicott's writing, rich with ideas based upon observation and experience as well as upon conjecture and speculation. Winnicott produces little by way of firm data: like much that is written by analysts and therapists, cases are used as illustrations, but not as the actual evidence from which he has made deductions. It is difficult for

academic psychologists to find in Winnicott alone any data that
will support his theories. The *Journal of Child Psychology and
Psychiatry*, for example, where we might expect to locate
Winnicott's influence on current research, or his significance in
conceptual frameworks, shows little evidence to confirm our
expectation. Unusually in volume 33 there are two articles, one on
object attachments, and another from the Winnicott Research Unit
on postnatal depression and infant development (Murray, 1992:
543–61); but this is not so in other volumes. Winnicott published in
the journal twice – his paper on 'String' (Winnicott, 1965b: 153–7)
appeared originally in the first volume (1960: 49–52); and he later
contributed in volume 4 (1963: 85–91) to a debate upon training
for child psychiatry (see below). However, in their 1986 'selective
review' of thirty years of child psychology, Clarke and Clarke make
no mention whatsoever of him (1986: 719–59). This is typical of
the absence of allusion to his work in academic journals. Com-
menting on why there might be this shunning of Winnicott by this
particular part of the academic world, Professor John Davis thinks
that he may be regarded as an advocate of sentimentality, in much
the same way as Freud was mistakenly regarded as the advocate of
sexuality. In fact Winnicott, Davis points out, could not stand
sentimentality, which he saw as the reverse side of sadism. He also
suggests that a reason for Winnicott's unpopularity amongst
academic psychologists is his concentration upon the individual as
unique, rather than upon statistical studies of groups (personal
communication).

This paucity of reference belies the fact that Winnicott's ideas can
be drawn upon for psychological research, and in some cases can be
empirically tested. Perhaps the prime (although not the only)
example of the development of Winnicott's work from an academic
perspective – fleshing out and testing his ideas with controlled
samples, precise observation, rigorous analysis and statistical
probity – is to be found in the projects undertaken by the
Winnicott Research Unit in the Department of Psychiatry in the
University of Cambridge, a particularly suitable location given
Winnicott's own links with Cambridge as a schoolboy and as an
undergraduate.

After her death Clare Winnicott left money for the establishment
of the Winnicott Trust, which in turn, as one of its initiatives,
financed a research fellowship in Cambridge. The Trust's aim was
to encourage empirical research on areas of concern to Winnicott,
and the then Chairman of the Trust, the late Dr Martin James,
decided that a university-based post would enable Dr Lynne
Murray to pursue her interest in turning Winnicott's essentially

descriptive work into a more scientific form. Her doctoral thesis on very early mother–infant communication had been influenced by Winnicott's thinking, and in her own training Murray had found a 'yawning gap' in the academic literature about emotional development in the very early months. Only attachment theory picked the themes up, and then only in the second half of the first year. She recognized how Winnicott's work really filled that gap, particularly for the study of normal development, while some of Klein's theory was particularly suitable for pathological situations and breakdown.

Her special concern has been looking at Winnicott's description of 'primary maternal preoccupation', and what this might mean for an infant's development. If Winnicott is right, that in the early weeks of life a baby needs to have the mother's sole attention through which she is able to provide an environment that facilitates the baby's development, then it should be possible to study a situation where primary maternal preoccupation may not occur in the normal way, for example mothers experiencing post-natal depression. In collaboration with others in Cambridge showing related concerns, Dr Murray was awarded a prize from Birthright, the research arm of the Royal College of Obstetricians and Gynaecologists. This financed a treatment trial to see if psychotherapeutic intervention with depressed mothers having difficulty with their babies could be effective in preventing some of the problems that can later arise in babies.

As a result of a benefaction in 1990 from the Tedworth Charitable Trust the idea of a Unit arose. Its aims are to study the development of infants and children in order to determine how environmental influences and inter-personal relationships, in interaction with genetic endowment, influence individual characteristics, personality and vulnerability to physical and psychiatric disorder. Funding for particular projects, now carried out by a team of researchers, has also been obtained from the Medical Research Council, the Department of Health, the East Anglian Regional Health Authority, the Mental Health Foundation, the Child Growth Foundation and the Isaac Newton Trust.

At the time of writing research projects have included studies of maternal depression and infant development (which I describe more fully below), the prediction and treatment of post-natal depression, the influence of infant factors on maternal mood and infant outcome, the influence of post-natal depression on feeding and infant growth, the impact of maternal eating disorders on infant development, and the relationship between maternal interactive style and infant outcome. The various studies have also provided opportunities for assessing the importance of different factors in the mother–baby relationship, which have been the main elements identified for particular research.

Central to the task of the observer is looking at the environmental provision and the baby's experience of the external world, and examining what implications these have for inner experience. The Winnicott Research Unit continues work through close observation of mothers and children, of children together, and children alone. The Winnicott Trust provides financial support for the analysis of video-taped interactions of mothers and infants at various points in this eighteen-month period: the films are analysed in fine detail, informed by theoretical constructs. The earliest work of the Unit involved a cohort of babies of depressed and non-depressed mothers originally recruited in 1986–8 and studied until they were eighteen months old. The original infants have been followed up, with their emotional, social and cognitive development assessed in school, at home and in the Unit playroom. One finding from the follow-up studies is that children whose mothers have had post-natal depression are less likely to make a positive approach to teachers in school. Boys of five, where there is a history of such maternal post-natal depression, have been shown to have significantly higher rates of behavioural problems in adjusting to school. Other studies have shown how the quality of responsiveness in the infant in the early weeks also powerfully influences maternal mood. One example of the relevance of this research, which supports Winnicott's theory of the mirroring function of the mother, is that poor infant motor control (either inert and flaccid or jerky and unmodulated) has been found to have a marked influence on the achievement of eye-to-eye contact, making it hard for parents to have the sense of relating to their infant, and diminishing the amount of 'inter-personal looking' (Murray et al., 1994b).

Research into the internal world of an infant (who is not, like many adults, able to describe their inner experience) may seem a very difficult task, although Dr Murray believes that it is possible to make inferences, and to develop tests to assess, for example, the recognition of self and other (in Winnicott's words, 'me and not me'). Strong relationships between mother and baby can be measured: there are, for example, indicators of when a mother is more preoccupied with her baby than with herself. Maternal behaviour can be rated on dimensions of sensitive–insensitive, accepting–demanding; or infants can be rated, using such dimensions as 'attentive–avoidant', 'contented–distressed' (Murray et al., 1994a). Predictions can be made about a baby's ability to distinguish self and other at nine months and eighteen months.

Practical Applications

These observations have led to treatment trials in Cambridge that are now in a position to inform clinical practice, particularly in the care of mothers and infants. Women identified as post-natally depressed have been offered a brief course of treatment in their own homes. They are assessed before and after treatment and regularly thereafter. They are then visited on approximately eight weekly occasions for hourly sessions. For this purpose health visitors have been trained in and supervised for short-term work – they bring to this work, of course, considerable prior experience of working with mothers and babies. Whilst improvement in maternal mood is important, the principal aim of the study is to ascertain whether treatment can improve the mother–infant relationship and so assist infant developmental outcome.

The original clinical trial was run with the random assignment of women to three different types of treatment: non-directive person-centred counselling; cognitive-behaviour therapy; and brief psycho-dynamic therapy, the latter aimed at promoting an understanding of the mother's representations of her infant, and her relationship with him or her, in terms of the mother's own early history and experience of being mothered. A control group was also included in the study. They received routine primary care but had no additional input from the research team. The bulk of the treatment was carried out by two health visitors and a psychotherapist, each of whom employed two different forms of treatment – this was to allow a control for the personal effect of the therapist. But a further control element was introduced by using specialists in some cases – a non-directive counsellor, a cognitive-behaviour therapist and an analytic therapist.

The trials show that it is possible to speed up recovery from post-natal depression through brief intervention, although it appears to make little difference which of the three methods is used. Those who received treatment fared significantly better than the untreated group in such areas as dealing with the infant's demands for attention, separation from the baby, playing with the baby, as well as the mother–infant relationship generally. The cognitive-behavioural approach produced the best outcome in these particular respects.

Following on from this research the Unit has been engaged in what is known as the Cambridge Intervention Study (Seeley et al., 1995). Health visitors are trained weekly for six half-days, with core items in the course involving learning about depression, and the impact of depression on the family, the use of the Edinburgh

Postnatal Depression Scale, basic counselling skills using Egan's model of Active Reflective Listening and selected techniques derived from cognitive-behaviour theory. Results from this study mirror those of the earlier treatment trial: there is significant improvement reported in maternal mood and the mother's perception of her relationship with her infant, as well as in the infant's behaviour.

Murray and Cooper (1993) describe at some length a case in which they treated a mother who found it difficult to feel closeness to her baby, and whose baby showed avoidance–attachment to her mother. They used a procedure largely based upon Bowlby's five principles for the application of attachment theory to adult psychtherapy (Bowlby, 1988), although they concentrated on the mother–child relationship (the child was in the room) rather than on the transference to themselves. The changes that took place in the mother, through being able to talk about her own childhood, and in experiencing feelings about that (which her twenty-month old child also witnessed) were reflected in the change in attachment behaviour in her child, which became much more secure.

Such interventions in the mother–baby relationship using attachment theory are not unique (Nezworski et al., 1988; Lieberman et al., 1991), and it is obvious that it is Bowlby who is the reference point here rather than Winnicott. Winnicott and Bowlby did not entirely agree about attachment, the former emphasizing the making, and the latter the breaking, of the mother–infant dyad. Neither did Winnicott altogether like the idea of introducing animal ethology into the study of human relationships (John Davis, personal communication). Nevertheless this research and the clinical trials are based upon Winnicott's recognition of the cardinal importance of the mother–baby dyad (or in Winnicott's phrase 'the nursing couple'), and their almost symbiotic relationship. Bowlby is particularly significant since, as Murray explains, 'in recent years, the influence of ethology, with its emphasis on the role of emotion in regulating interactions, coupled with detailed descriptive work, has to some extent bridged the gap [between psychoanalysis and developmental psychology]' (Murray, 1989). In her article in the *British Journal of Psychotherapy* (1989) Murray sets side by side terms used to describe developments in the first year of life, by developmental psychologists on the one hand and Winnicott and Klein on the other. Detailed observation of infants, as described in Chapter 4 with reference to Daniel Stern, has led to the need to qualify some of Winnicott's ideas – for example, the theory of primary unintegration. Nevertheless, other evidence from research into neonatal behaviour appears to show some support for

Winnicott's concept of the undifferentiated self and the external world, and for the stress laid in object relations theory upon the relation of mother to baby as a whole (that is, in all its qualities and not just in respect of satisfaction of physical drives). Observation of mothers and infants in the first year has also in some cases convincingly lent support to Winnicott's ideas about primary maternal preoccupation, the mirror role of the mother, and the mother's adaptation to the changing needs of the infant at about three months by introducing the external world in small doses.

While the work of the Winnicott Research Unit is regularly reported in articles in scientific journals, Winnicott's name, as I have indicated above, seldom appears in articles in psychology journals. Perhaps through the careful work of the Winnicott Research Unit, and a few researchers in other universities, Winnicott's observations from a lifetime's clinical experience may be seen as capable of objective analysis through empirical tests and therefore worthy of further investigation.

Paediatrics

Paediatrics in England has a long tradition of offering a free service to the children of poor families; even before Winnicott there was recognition that 'if you separate a child from its mother you break its heart immediately' (John Davis, personal communication). It was this speciality that Winnicott chose to enter, and much of the evidence as well as the sheer volume of his data for his theoretical position came from this setting. He was, of course, more of a psychiatrist than a physician in his paediatric clinics, although in the spatula game Winnicott developed a technique for assessment that demonstrated not just psychological but also neurological development. As his one-time colleague in paediatrics John Davis says, 'in a half a minute you can find out everything you want to about a baby, by handing it a spatula' (personal communication).

Winnicott became excluded from the way paediatrics developed, even though John Davis and Sir Peter Tizard encouraged the brightest and most interested young paediatricians working with them at the Hammersmith Hospital to attend seminars in Winnicott's home. This action, Clare Winnicott felt, saved him from feeling cut off, although as the next section shows, she herself took Winnicott and his work into the world of social work where some of his ideas were indeed taken up. On the other hand paediatrics has not gone at all in the direction of Winnicott, and what he had to offer has largely been lost to present paediatric practice. His former colleague Professor John Davis sees it as nothing less than a 'tragedy, that he was not at the heart of the paediatric profession from the beginning' (personal communication).

In an address from his position of chair of the Medical Section of the British Psychological Society Winnicott sought to show the necessity for co-operation between the two disciplines of paediatrics and psychiatry: 'the research worker in each of the two specialities has much to gain by meeting the research worker in the other' (1975: 158). In practice, however, it is difficult to find paediatricians (who tend to be oriented to the physical dimension) co-operating on equal terms with child therapists (who are oriented towards problems in emotional development and relationships). The division between child psychiatrists and paediatricians is exacerbated by the former tending to come to their speciality via psychiatry rather than via paediatrics. In a debate on the issue of the training of child psychiatrists in the *Journal of Child Psychology and Psychiatry* (1963: 85–91; see also Winnicott, 1965b: 193–202), Winnicott shows how he did not believe general psychiatry could be trusted to represent child psychology. He sees the latter as a speciality in its own right, and he wants to open the route to child psychiatry from paediatrics. Hersov, reviewing developments in child psychiatry over a thirty year period to 1986, comments that 'the dust still has not settled completely on this issue even today, and there are still those who hold that the required training in general psychiatry frightens off paediatricians who would make excellent child psychiatrists' (1986: 790).

Hersov's article (unlike Clarke and Clarke, 1986, on child psychology) shows that Winnicott has been influential in child psychiatry, although 'his style was often copied, but never equalled and his ideas seemed to have more to offer to social workers than to others' (Hersov, 1986: 788). It is in the United States, amongst analytically-oriented child development researchers, that his concepts of the mother–infant relationship have attracted increasing attention. Stern, for example, refers to Winnicott several times in his important book on infant development, one which takes the twin perspectives of developmental psychology and psychoanalysis. He assigns particular value to Winnicott's ideas: of the infant's need for 'going on being'; of early language and sounds as a transitional phenomenon; of the development of a false self; and his list of primitive agonies in the infant's experience, 'whenever temporary and partial dissolutions of the sense of a core self occur' (Stern, 1985: 123, 173–4, 199–200, 202, 210). In place of true self and false self, Stern suggests the adoption of a tri-partite vocabulary: the social self, the private self and the disavowed self (1985: 229).

It might be expected, given his immense experience of child psychotherapy, in public and private settings, that Winnicott would be influential in child psychotherapy training. In fact, in London where the Kleinian (at the Tavistock) and the Freudian (at the Hampstead Clinic) trainings vie with each other, Winnicott scarcely gets a mention. There is marginal interest in him on the British Association of Psychotherapists child therapy course. Farhi suggests (personal communication) that Winnicott has to be seen in an historical context in which Klein was predominant, and in which he was consciously trying to undermine the Kleinian grip on language and understanding. This may still affect the way his work is regarded in the most orthodox settings. Lomas writes (personal communication) that 'perhaps Winnicott has paid a price for not standing out – as he should – more forcibly against Klein. To me he has a far greater stature and is fundamentally different.' Nevertheless outside London, for example in the Scottish Institute of Human Relations training in child psychotherapy in Edinburgh, or the School of Child and Adolescent Psychoanalytical Psychotherapy in Rome, his work is respected and taught.

Winnicott's Influence in the United States

Although Winnicott was received with much criticism in New York when he delivered his paper 'The Use of an Object' (see Chapter 1), there is considerable interest in his work in the United States, in Europe and in other parts of the world. Winnicott visited America several times and delivered papers to various analytic societies in a number of states. Rodman, the editor of Winnicott's letters *The Spontaneous Gesture* (1987), is one of the leading advocates of Winnicott's work, although there are others, such as Grolnick (Grolnick et al., 1978; Grolnick 1990), who co-edited one of the earliest studies devoted entirely to Winnicott, and Grotstein (1994), who writes on Winnicott as well as Bion (Grotstein, 1981). Orthodox American psychoanalysis has always tended towards ego psychology and the work (amongst others) of Anna Freud, rather than Klein; but Chodorow, in a note to her introduction to *Feminism and Psychoanalytic Theory*, states that 'for perhaps the first time in the history of American psychoanalysis, synthetic and inclusionary tendencies seem to be more dominant than sectarian and exclusionary tendencies' (1989: 222). As an illustration of this she writes that 'in the journals, Winnicott is almost mainstream'.

Many of the articles from psychoanalytic journals cited in Chapter 4 show the lively interest there is in some of Winnicott's ideas – particularly transitional phenomena and objects, and the positive connotations given to the concept of illusion (for example Eigen, 1981; Bronstein, 1992). Furthermore there is some common ground, with regard to object relations theory and child development, between Winnicott and Margaret Mahler (Mahler et al., 1975), René Spitz (1965), Daniel Stern (1985 – and see pp. 107, 129) and others. Harold Searles clearly finds Winnicott's ideas on illusion and the mother–baby relationship invaluable for his own paper on 'Scorn, Disillusionment and Adoration in the Psychotherapy of Schizophrenia' (1965: 605–25), and comments favourably too on Winnicott's identification of hatred in the mother and in the therapist (1965: 527). Greenberg and Mitchell state that Winnicott's theory of the emergence of the self provides a foundation for developmental theory 'radically different from that of his Freudian and Kleinian predecessors' (1983: 188).

A number of American authors in the fields of literature and history accord Winnicott a central place in the development of psychoanalytic ideas. Hughes (1989) includes him as one of the three figures (the others being Fairbairn and Klein) who have been instrumental in 'reshaping the psychoanalytic domain'; of the three, Hughes believes that Winnicott did most to describe the concept of the mother, and to describe the analytic environment. Rudnytsky's study (1991) of the major figures in psychoanalysis since Freud concentrates upon Rank and Winnicott. In one chapter he also contrasts Winnicott, Lacan and Kohut and declares his own bias:

> Any attempt to come to terms with Freud must take the measure of him both as a human being and as a thinker. By the same token, when I now ask where psychoanalysis can go after Freud . . . I am in one respect announcing my search for a figure to whom I can have a transference as intense and satisfying as that aroused by Freud. I have found that figure in Winnicott. (1991: 71)

These are academics who are aware that they are making subjective judgements, but such studies, comparing and contrasting him with other major figures, demonstrate the growing interest there is in Winnicott in some disciplines in American academic life.

Winnicott, Lacan and France

The intellectual framework of psychoanalysis in France is radically different from that in America, but Winnicott has clearly made an impact in some quarters there. Clancier and Kalmanovitch conclude their book on *Winnicott and Paradox* with interviews with several French psychoanalysts (1987: 105–50). Winnicott had visited Paris as a guest of child analysts as early as 1949, and returned to France several times, for example addressing the Conférence des Psych-analyses de Langues Romanes in Paris in 1954 on 'Withdrawal and Regression' (1975: 255–61). In 1953 he was part of a small committee looking at the question of membership of the International Psychoanalytic Association for the break away Société Française de Psychanalyse (which included Lacan). He is also known through Pontalis's translations of some of his articles for the *Nouvelle Revue de Psychanalyse*, and of the book *Playing and Reality*. *Human Nature* and Rodman's collection of Winnicott's letters in *The Spontaneous Gesture* have also been translated.

Winnicott's relationship with Lacan is an interesting one. It led to some correspondence (Winnicott invited Lacan to London in 1960, although Lacan could not make space for a visit), and later to some difficulties for Winnicott. Like Lacan, Winnicott was a non-conformist, with a creative mind, and a member (Rycroft sees him as the unofficial leader) of the 'middle group' in psychoanalysis which, if it did not split off from the mainstream British society, did not lose its sense of independence either. Such were their similarities. In some ways they were very different, in their style of writing, and indeed in their thinking. Nevertheless they were interested in each other's ideas. In the sixties, Winnicott's position as president of the British Psycho-Analytical Society made it difficult for him to run the risk of appearing to endorse the Lacanians, so he declined an invitation to visit. Instead he contributed a paper that could be read at a colloquium on childhood psychoses in Paris in 1967. It was the same year that Winnicott wrote his paper on the mirror role of the mother (1971a: 111–18), inspired by, but as it turned out, radically different from Lacan (see Chapter 2).

The translation of Winnicott's writings at about that time had 'considerable impact' on three of the French societies, the Association Psychanalytique de France, the École Freudienne de Paris and the more orthodox Société Psychanalytique de Paris (Roudinesco, 1990: 491). Roudinesco also comments that in the 1970s Lacanian therapists of the fourth generation discovered the existence of ideas to which they had previously been deaf, such as 'the work of D. W. Winnicott . . . which . . . brought a sense of clinical practice capable of serving as a counterweight to dogmatic Lacanianism at a time when a generalized opening toward pluralism was dominating the French psychoanalytic scene' (Roudinesco, 1990: 465). The French analyst André Green, sometime Freud Professor of Psycho-analysis in London, has suggested that some of Lacan's disciples have moved in Winnicott's direction since Lacan's death (Clancier and Kalmanovitch, 1987: 121). He has himself inherited much from Winnicott's thinking.

All the French analysts who agreed to be interviewed by Clancier speak highly of Winnicott's work, and warmly of the value they assign to some of his concepts, although it is also obvious that his thinking and writing does not easily sit with the tendency of French theoretical systems to be well-structured and well-organized. 'The most striking formulas are not necessarily based on the most rigorous epistemology,' comments one of them (Clancier and Kalmanovitch, 1987: 118; references in this and the next two paragraphs are all to this book). J.-B. Pontalis summarizes his and perhaps others' responses by saying that 'one can trace back Freud's thought, one can expound Melanie Klein's theory, one can systematize Lacan's theories even more. If you try to do that with Winnicott, you lose what is best of him' (1987: 143). Another person comments that in France Winnicott is an antidote to 'rather intellectualist formalism' (1987: 145).

It is above all his open-mindedness and his creativity that are valued even if one of those interviewed observed that 'there can hardly be a school of open-mindedness' (1987: 118). This makes for another reason why it is difficult to speak of a 'Winnicottian': 'for a long time, thank God, Winnicott was not a Winnicottian' (1987: 118 – does this imply that this commentator thinks eventually he was?). Pontalis admires not so much his concepts – as he points out, 'anybody can produce concepts' – as 'the intuition that underlies that concept [the transitional object]' (1987: 139). Another analyst comments similarly that Winnicott's theories are 'pretty lame ones', but that in this they are 'like all psychoanalytic theories' (1987: 119). Nevertheless his writing about the true and the false self, illusion, the transitional object and transitional space, if somewhat overstated by Winnicott himself, or exaggerated in their importance by some of those who follow him, finds echoes in some French psychoanalytic thought. Indeed, André Green accords Winnicott a significant place in the history of psychoanalysis, with the comment that after Freud two authors, Lacan and Winnicott, 'pushed their research and coherence very far on the basis of two quite different points of view, and . . . up to a certain point converge' (1987: 121).

What these leading French analysts particularly praise is Winnicott's ability in conferences and other meetings to reflect deeply within himself and then to make highly pertinent comments. A number of them are clearly also impressed by their observation of his consultations with children using the squiggle game and play, even with children whose language he did not speak. His use of himself, his authenticity and his intuitive understanding of the needs of the psychotic patient receive similar affirmation. Yet one person wisely comments that the problem with the squiggle game is 'you need Winnicott's own genius and creativity to make it work. If one tried to imitate it, it would be transmitted magic, a mere conjuring trick' (1987: 131). Another speaks of 'the risk that some people have been able to interpret Winnicott's works as an authorization of a kind of spontaneism, whereas in him there was a very profound knowledge of psychoanalytic technique and practice' (1987: 147).

Other European analysts similarly refer positively to Winnicott's contribution to psychoanalysis. Nikolaas Treurniet (1993) in the Netherlands is one such author, and I have already drawn in Chapter 4 on the work of two Italian analysts, Usuelli (1992) and Mancia (1993). The Gaddinis (1970) also deserve mention, particularly for their study of the prevalence of the transitional object in different social groups. Mancia links Winnicott with Klein as one of the two figures to whom contemporary psychoanalysis is 'much indebted' (1993: 941). Winnicott's tradition has been taught in the Neuropsichiatria Infantile of Rome University since the mid-1970s, with the encouragement of Masud Khan, Clare Winnicott and Marion Milner, and it spread to Milan in the 1990s. Most of his work, translated by Renata Gaddini, has been published in Italy, and links have been forged with the Squiggle Foundation (see below). Similar interest in Winnicott through the Squiggle Foundation has grown in demand, not only in France, Italy and the United States, but in Australia, New Zealand, Israel, Sweden, the Republic of Ireland and South America. Some of these countries have established centres related to the Squiggle Foundation, to further the study of Winnicott's work.

Winnicott in Britain

In Britain a number of major writers on psychoanalytic theory and technique are obviously informed and often inspired by Winnicott. Masud Khan, his one-time analysand, the first editor of Winnicott's papers, and a provocative author in his own right (see 1974; 1983 for example), could not be more fulsome in his praise: he writes, in the concluding phrase of his brilliant and concise summary of Winnicott's work, that he 'was one such the like of whom I shall not meet again' (Winnicott, 1975: xlviii). In introducing Khan's chapter in *Between Reality and Fantasy* (Grolnick et al., 1978: 257), one of the editors describes Khan's work as using 'a therapeutic stance derived from an understanding of play and the role of the nonintrusive mother in creating a holding, facilitating, nurturing environment'. Cooper's study of Khan, uncannily similar in its structure to the editor's plan for this series, provides a useful way into Khan's work and describes more fully his relationship with Winnicott (Cooper, 1993).

Marion Milner writes (Grolnick et al., 1978: 39) of how much she gained from Winnicott's concept of the holding environment, even embodying the idea in the title of her book *In the Hands of the Living God* (1969; see also Milner, 1957). It was after hearing Winnicott lecture that she decided to train as an analyst, and she regularly attended his study groups. Her weekly presence at seminars in the Squiggle Foundation has provided a real sense of continuity between a generation that knew Winnicott in person, and a new generation of teachers and therapists who know him only through his writing. Margaret Little (1981; 1990) owed much to Winnicott for the way he held her through her psychotic breakdown while in analysis with him. She describes herself as one of those 'who mainly approve or agree [but] also have serious points of difference with him'. She continues:

> Perhaps the chief outcome of this is the very width of his impact on the 'total field', where ideas that he first put forward have been quietly appropriated and accepted without being attributed to him, and often attributed elsewhere. (Little, 1990: 114–15)

Like others she calls him a genius, although not of the first order (1990: 118). The image she adopts is of Winnicott as 'yeast' that 'will live and grow for a long, long time' (1990: 119).

Frances Tustin (Spensley, 1994) is another analyst and writer for whom Winnicott's work has been a central feature, and who has herself done much to further his approach through her interest in and commitment to the Squiggle Foundation. Her writing on autism and psychotic states of mind in children (1986; 1990; 1992 for example) has been described as shining 'a brilliant light into a normally impenetrable darkness' (Riley, 1993: 76). She gives renewed stress to the critical importance of detailed observation of children before making statements about early development. She expands areas of exploration that can be identified with Winnicott: the relation between internal and external realities, play, symbolic and transitional activity, creativity, the psychosomatic nature of primitive experience and the prolonged dependence of the human infant. Like Winnicott she 'does not rely on psychoanalytic jargon. She writes beautifully clear and evocative language, sometimes drawing on poetry and pictures to convey her meaning, at other times organizing her thoughts in a disciplined and rigorous manner' (Riley, 1993: 83). Margaret Little and Frances Tustin died within weeks of each other during the time this book was written. Each gave generous bequests to the Squiggle Foundation.

Of the 'middle group' of psychoanalysts who are influenced by him, Charles Rycroft perhaps owes more to Fairbairn than Winnicott. He agrees that he uses 'very similar concepts to Winnicott's, but I like to think that I understand symbolism better than he did and that I am not so soppy' (Rycroft, 1985: 20). Nevertheless, I have already quoted in Chapter 4 Rycroft's assessment of Winnicott's 'concept of a transitional reality, which mediates between the private world of dreams and the public, shared world of the environment, [as] perhaps the most important contribution made to psychoanalytical theory in the last thirty years', even if it is not entirely original (Rycroft, 1985: 145). His debt to Winnicott and Milner is acknowledged in Fuller's introduction to Rycroft's *Psychoanalysis and Beyond* (1985: 24, 36), and he himself writes that he was 'appalled by the struggle Winnicott had in order to get a proper hearing' in the British Psycho-Analytical Society (1985: 206).

Peter Lomas, at one time another of the 'middle group', adapts one of Winnicott's phrases for the title of his *True and False Experience* (1973), and acknowledges in various places that Winnicott has made an 'invaluable' contribution to the creation of a 'facilitating environment' in therapy itself, or to the understanding of 'therapeutic breakdown'. As I have described in Chapter 4 Lomas is critical of some of Winnicott's ideas about practice, and finds confusion in some of his ideas, but he also acknowledges how 'many therapists, including myself, [are] indebted to him' (1987a: 83); and a little later he observes that 'his imaginative writings have played a part in encouraging practitioners to adopt a more relaxed therapeutic stance in general' (1987a: 93).

Other British writers who follow in the steps of Winnicott's imaginative interpretation of psychoanalytic ideas include Christopher Bollas (1987; 1992; 1995). His adaptation of 'transitional object' to include the concept of the 'transformational object', an object or symbol which assists psychic change, is one example of his highly original thinking. One reviewer describes Bollas' work in terms of its 'poetics . . . imagination . . . creativity . . . and elaborations of psychoanalytic thought and practice' (Grotstein, 1994: 56). Adam Phillips, author of the Fontana Masters volume on Winnicott, is another writer of similar originality in his developing work, and his impish titles (such as *On Kissing, Tickling and Being Bored*, 1993, and *On Flirtation*, 1994) partly recall Winnicott's playfulness. Each of course stands in his own right, yet it is appropriate that both these last-named writers have served on the editorial board of *Winnicott Studies*, the journal of the Squiggle Foundation.

Social Work

Winnicott's war-time experience as consultant psychiatrist to the government evacuation scheme in Oxfordshire was, according to the editors of *Deprivation and Delinquency* (Winnicott, 1984), a 'watershed [for] . . . the broadening and flowering of his theory of development' (1984: 9). Children were 'disturbed' in the sense of initially having their expectations of stable provision disturbed through their evacuation from their families. Winnicott's particular experience was gained through working with deprived children who had become delinquent and needed special provision, since they could not settle in ordinary homes. Clare Britton (later to be his second wife) joined his team as a psychiatric social worker and administrator of five children's hostels. If Winnicott's thinking and practice received a whole new dimension, Clare describes how 'his thinking actually affected what went on in the hostels, and how children were treated by individual staff members' (Winnicott, 1984: 3).

This was the start of Winnicott's (although perhaps in this context I ought also to say the two Winnicotts') influence on social work, especially upon child care. Pietroni and Poupard describe how 'generations of social workers and social work teachers have been influenced in the use of constructive play, to enable children to communicate fantasies, wishes and anxieties by Clare and Donald Winnicott' (1991: 78). They particularly refer to Hendry's paper (1987), which shows how the therapeutic communication with children that the Winnicotts came to represent 'can be used in a modern social services context to help distressed children through difficult transitions'.

If we are looking for areas outside psychoanalysis where Winnicott's work helps to inform other literature, it is most notable in this field of child care. Whether writing about residential child care, fostering and adoption, child protection, working with families, or delinquency, the British still continue to refer to many of his key concepts. One recent example among many is Varma (1992) on *The Secret Life of Vulnerable Children*.

It is important not to forget Clare Winnicott in her own right as a teacher and an author (although less prolific than her husband). She introduced a particularly useful tool in communicating with children which she called 'the indirect approach' or 'the third object': 'it helps to have something between us and the child, a third thing going on, which at any moment can become a focal point to relieve tension' (1968: 70–1). This may be a ride in a car, a walk, drawing, playing, or even watching television together. Clare

Winnicott later became a lecturer on the Applied Social Studies course at the London School of Economics, and in 1963 was appointed Director of Child Care Studies at the Home Office Children's Department, where she was responsible for the organization and oversight of training courses for residential staff and child care officers. Her papers are collected in *Child Care and Social Work* (1964).

During the Second World War, in the neighbouring county of Berkshire but independently of Winnicott in Oxfordshire, Barbara Dockar-Drysdale had started a play-group, called 'the Mulberry Bush' after such a tree in the garden of the house where the play-group met. It evolved into a nursery school in her own home: 'at that time there were many mothers and children in difficulties caused by wartime conditions, so that soon we collected several mothers and their children to live with us in addition to our own family' (1968: xiii). A chain of circumstances led to the foundation of a residential school for disturbed children, 'the Mulberry Bush School', which was financially supported by the Ministry of Education, and professionally supported by a number of specialists in child care from different disciplines. At the same time Barbara Dockar-Drysdale trained as a psychotherapist. The return of her husband from war service meant that he could take over administration in the school while she could develop its therapeutic work. Later she became a consultant to a number of similar projects.

It was not until the 1950s, after addressing the British Association of Scientists on the care of what she called 'frozen children', that she met the Winnicotts, and thereafter her writing reflects their (and particularly D. W. W's) influence. Their converging paths also informed Winnicott. He liked the term 'frozen child', preferring it to the more clinical description of 'the affectionless child'. The frozen child is 'the tragic outcome of a disrupted unity, where the baby has been separated from its mother for one of many causes'; the 'frozen' child implies that 'a thaw can follow a frost' (Dockar-Drysdale, 1968: 17). She observes that a frozen child, upon referral, may steal food because he wants food at that moment, and for no other reason. When the same child is beginning to recover he may steal food again, but because the therapist is absent: the stealing becomes symbolic.

She also refers to 'archipelago children', who have achieved the first steps towards integration, but 'one could describe them as ego-islets which have never fused into a continent – a total person' (1968: 99–100). They have a limited capacity for symbolization, which facilitates communication, although, as Winnicott observes in his foreword to her book, 'six people meet a child and seem to see six different children' (1968: ix). Her third category of disturbed child picks up Winnicott's phrase of the 'false self' (1968: 100–1). His influence is also seen in the full title of her book *Provision of the Primary Experience: Winnicottian Work with Children and Adolescents* (1990), the first chapter of which is titled 'My Debt to Winnicott' – an account of her monthly meetings with him over a period of seventeen years.

Winnicott and Dockar-Drysdale are both acknowledged as informing the work of 'Womankind', a women's mental health project in Bristol. Barbara Dockar-Drysdale has been their visiting consultant. Pamela Trevithick, in Ferguson et al. (1993), describes her work with two women who have experienced childhood abuse, and draws not only upon a feminist perspective but also upon Winnicott in her understanding of trauma. She sets out the approach of 'Womankind' as

> exploring ways of incorporating and adapting Winnicott and Dockar-Drysdale into our group work and individual counselling sessions . . . The common thread that runs through all our work is the importance given to the use of transitional phenomena, including transitional objects and experiences, as an aid to recovery and self-cure. Here we stress the importance of 'reliability and consistency' and 'adaptation to need', because together these form part of the facilitating environment in which self-cure can take place. (Ferguson et al., 1993: 123)

The Squiggle Foundation

In the mid-1970s Alexander Newman, a family care worker in Camden, London, was struck by the lack of provision for training, support and supervision for people working with young families. He quickly saw the importance of Winnicott's work for other family care workers, and started a series of meetings that would not only help place these workers in a theoretical framework, but would also in itself provide a facilitating, containing structure. At that point Newman had no specifically psychoanalytic training, although he later went on to train as a Jungian analyst. His knowledge of Winnicott was profound, but while he had corresponded with Winnicott, they had never met.

Within a few years the courses which Newman started had begun to attract many therapists, although, as the present director has observed, these people already had considerable provision: 'there has always existed a creative tension between responding to those who already have acquired an appetite and those others who have a "low quality" of an internalized model of desire' (Farhi, personal communication). There was always at the beginning a great desire to bring in teachers, doctors and social workers. These meetings took the form of Newman speaking on a theme from Winnicott, just from notes (he was very creative), followed by lunch and discussion. There were 36 Saturday seminars annually, always different each year. Other people, such as Nina Farhi, who is the present director of the Foundation, were then asked to take particular seminars. There were also six public lectures a year given by 'the great luminaries': Masud Khan, Marion Milner, Frances Tustin, Kenneth Lambert, Hannah Segal – a list which represents the broad spectrum of theoretical approaches, including Jungians and Kleinians, that were and still are drawn within the ambit of the Foundation. The somewhat small group who then gave those lectures has since been considerably extended in the programming of the bi-monthly public lectures that continue to attract a large audience. The subjects are not confined to Winnicott's ideas, although sometimes they take him as a starting point. Alexander Newman and John Fielding were the first editors of *Winnicott Studies*, the journal of the Squiggle Foundation, which originally almost totally reproduced the public lectures and some of the seminars. This journal later incorporated other papers and reviews, although in 1995 it changed its format, into single books on particular themes published by Karnac Books.

Nina Farhi became Director in 1989, at which time she set about providing a more formal structure that could contain growth, together with a constitution, membership (about 250 at the time of writing), trustees and a salaried part-time general secretary (33 Amberley Road, London N13 4BH). The new director consolidated and stabilized the basis of the Squiggle Foundation's work, returning to the original aim of offering courses to family care workers and others working outside the more narrow field of psychotherapy. There is now a rather more structured syllabus for the Saturday seminars, called 'Original themes in the work of D. W. Winnicott': the first term is largely about concepts of health, the second term looks at issues around health and pathology such as true and false self and psyche–soma, and the third is centred on the themes of creativity and playing. Tapes are made of these seminars and are available in an extensive tape library. About forty people are accepted on the seminar course each year, some of the places being assisted through bursaries. There is also a Madeleine Davis Bursary each year for a particularly able student, who could not otherwise afford the course. True to the original aim of the Foundation, the Saturday seminar members include young family care workers, residential social workers, psychiatric nurses, midwives, psychologists, GPs, community workers, art, drama and music therapists, musicians, poets, writers as well as psychotherapists and psychoanalysts. It is not a psychotherapy training course, which makes it perhaps more pleasurable and more creative than many trainings tend to be (with all the baggage of assessment and in some cases their commitment to a particular theoretical position).

In addition the Squiggle Foundation runs a series of seminars for further study: the membership is smaller, open to anyone involved with children and adults in any work setting. In the 'Further Studies' group Winnicott's texts are more closely examined and related to clinical work, and the third term looks at people who have been influenced by Winnicott. The 'Clinical Issues' group is limited to eight members, arising out of the request from many people for supervision. It is not in fact a supervision group, but rather one where the theoretical underpinning of psychoanalysis is looked at from Winnicott's writings, or from people influenced by him. Critical attention is brought to bear upon clinical practice. There is also a resource group of people who know his work very well, but who meet to argue and examine critically the validity of Winnicott's ideas. This meets every six weeks, underpinning the work and informing the culture of the Squiggle Foundation itself, and feeding back into the quality and enjoyment of the teaching of the seminars. The director also runs special workshops, for residential social workers working with disturbed adolescents and for other specialized work groups.

Throughout these different levels of activity Winnicott's texts are not treated as sacred. Nina Farhi's fundamental understanding of Winnicott's work is that 'to have any meaning, value or vitality at all, theory has to be created by the person who inhabits it; if there were a canonical text, as it were, it would soon die a dubious and well-merited death' (personal communication). As director she, like Winnicott, hates dogma. She has no wish that Winnicott should be romanticized, recognizing how Winnicott can attract people in an idolatrous way. She wishes instead to disturb people through his work, and to assist people in creating their own text, theory and understanding.

Many London trainings in psychotherapy employ Squiggle teachers for the Winnicott part of their syllabus. It may even be said that Winnicott has got on to their syllabus because the high profile of the Foundation, which in psychoanalytic circles in London is perhaps unique in its broad spectrum and appeal. Squiggle also works out of London, mainly through day workshops in the provinces, consisting of two or three papers on health, on the development of pathology, and creativity and play, together with small work discussion groups. Its teachers are increasingly being invited abroad.

Conclusion

This study started out with the question why Winnicott, both in his person and in his particular expression of psychoanalytic thought and practice, should have exerted such a fascination for many counsellors and therapists. This chapter has expanded the initial observation that he tends to be a 'favourite' for many practitioners in the wider world of care and counselling, by showing the extent and degree of his influence, despite the more critical reception he received during his lifetime from a number of his eminent psychoanalytic colleagues. That original question about him should now be addressed in summarizing this chapter and this book.

Winnicott appeals because he is essentially an imaginative therapist and writer. He imagines his way into the experiences of therapy (through intuition more than feeling). Whether he writes about cases or concepts, he uses a combination of observations, standard terms, paradoxical and poetic phrasing to carry that imaginative argument along. Thus he can be convincing, even when other evidence suggests alternative explanations. Indeed, even if he is sometimes shown to be wrong (for example, that there *is* such a thing as a baby), the significance of his image remains. His phrasing is often metaphorical, but it is more than metaphor, perhaps because he does not see his terms as such. The forcefulness of his conviction and the playfulness of his words matches a desire in the reader that what he writes should indeed be so, even when the intellect knows that it may not be as straightforward as he at first makes it appear. Of course, on further reading, in the same text and elsewhere, the complexities begin to arise and lead to a different appreciation, this time one that recognizes both the strength of paradox and the weakness of contradiction. In his own terms we might even call reading him a process of illusionment and disillusionment, bearing in mind the positive connotations given by Winnicott to both terms.

Winnicott's imaginative style clearly resonates with a good number of his readers, and, probably because he lacks precision, he is able to resonate with different individuals in various ways. This can be his strength, especially if the individual is inspired through him to search for, if not always arrive at, her or his own position. Better this than to idolize Winnicott as a guru. If sometimes he, like many other analysts, is tempted to universalize, we also sense that he is content that different people might understand him in unique ways. After all 'no two infants are alike' (1965b: 49). He resonates with individual experience, but perhaps more so with individual imagination and fantasy, because he often describes experience which is either too early to verbalize, or is the subject of more imagining than information. If what he writes is not always scientifically verifiable (or even at times clearly not scientifically proven), it tends not to matter, at least as long as the reader remains aware of the particular status and limitations of his discourse: such imaginative expression, whether or not it is intuitively correct, can extend our ability to be in touch, or to believe that we are in touch with our own experience, as well as sometimes (but not of course always) with the experience of others.

A healthy response to Winnicott therefore helps us to extend our own imagination and to value our intuition more; to enjoy the opportunities for spontaneity; to play with ideas that spring to mind; to trust ourselves and not depend upon theories and techniques, however much they are put forward with rigour and vigour, as being applicable at all times and in all situations. While it may be the content of his work which at first attracts, what comes through in the end is the primacy of the ability to be both destructive and creative.

In wondering why there has been so much interest in Winnicott's idea of the transitional object, Flew makes a suggestion. He quotes an historian of ideas, 'that "influence" is not a simple, but on the contrary, a very complex bilateral relation. We are not influenced by everything we read or learn. In one sense, and perhaps the deepest, we ourselves determine the influences we are submitting to: our intellectual ancestors are by no means given to, but are freely chosen by us' (Flew, 1978: 485–6). Winnicott's ideas similarly may impress and excite because he speaks to 'antecedent concerns and beliefs' in us, without necessarily being accurate in the form in which he expresses them in his papers. In turn, Winnicott himself chose Darwin and Freud as the two major influences upon him in his youth, not necessarily for their intellectual arguments alone, but also because they appealed to something antecedent in him.

Flew's is a helpful suggestion. Winnicott concentrates upon a primary relationship which is particularly evocative, emotionally and historically, for all of us: the mother–baby couple. It is not just the subject but the manner in which he deals with the subject, and the style in which he describes his subject, that persuades us, even at times against our better judgement: largely undogmatic, generous in his descriptions, positive in his belief and caring in his manner, he is like the mother we would all have wished to have. There are of course dangers here: I have referred to idealization and romanticization as criticisms either of Winnicott or of some of those attracted to him. His picture of the human condition is not full enough, but we can see why it appeals.

Flew also suggests that there may also be something in the character and style of the man which appeals, even if his ideas are not always fully worked through (1978: 486). Those who read this book, and most of those who now write about Winnicott, including this author, never knew him. Even those who worked with him, or trained with him, are increasingly and inevitably fewer in number. There has arisen in this author nonetheless, in researching this book, the conviction that Winnicott, starting in his own childhood, and even to some extent arising from his adult life, was a person who was loved and who needed to be loved. This led, in the way he put forward his theories, both to wariness about losing favour with his peers – causing him at times to nod a little too deeply in the direction of received wisdom – and also to the wish to stand out and be distinctive, as he was in his family of origin. This results in what is in some ways an unfortunate double agenda, each part stemming from the same need to be appreciated, where he is not sure enough in himself either to argue his own position thoroughly, or to reject convincingly the tradition he wants to question.

Such speculation, and indeed a more thorough-going interpretation of the way he thought and felt about himself and others, must await the fuller biography of him which hopefully someone will eventually undertake. My own interpretation of him as someone who was loved and who needed to be loved is of course not exceptional, and indeed could apply to many people. Yet it may also be part of his appeal to the many therapists and counsellors who, in debates about psychoanalytic ideas, not surprisingly sit on the fence. Unlike their more dogmatic or intellectually convinced colleagues (particularly here I think of some analysts and psychotherapists), they try to combine holding on to a tradition which has initially moulded them, with their doubts about its certainty (see also Farhi, 1992). They too need to belong for the sake of their professional status, but they also want to question or even to rebel. Winnicott stands for someone who is both accepted and unconventional. Yet of course the more who are attracted to him for these reasons the greater the risk that there will be in psychotherapy and counselling, if it is the right collective term, a conformity of nonconformists.

What I suggest is not true of those who draw upon Winnicott as a means to find their own creativity and uniqueness. The Squiggle Foundation is a good example of this, as are many of the writers and therapists whom I have named in this chapter. Yet my interpretation may explain his appeal to that wider audience that dabbles in his work, adopts his phrases, and even calls itself 'Winnicottian'!

There is a danger that a book like this may fuel the idolization of a figure who is already England's most loved analyst. Winnicott is eminently quotable. His ideas can be fascinating. His interventions in therapy are at times startling. These last two chapters are essential to balance what may be a false impression conveyed by the first three. Taken at face value his thinking needs both closer examination and the type of criticism that it received while he was alive, which the generation after his death is in danger of forgetting. What is so heartening is to find that there are nonetheless therapists, teachers and writers who are building upon Winnicott's own mischievous spirit of iconoclasm, even more convincingly than he did, and who are inspired by his readiness to experiment with psychoanalytic language, method and concepts. It is this type of approach that provides hope for the critical identification and imaginative exploration of the many gaps that remain in our knowledge of nature, humankind and the therapeutic task, that Winnicott, like his contemporaries such as Klein or Bowlby, or his predecessors Darwin and Freud, has affirmed as potentially creative transitional space.

Select Bibliography of Winnicott's Works

The starting point for an initial study of Winnicott must be his most famous book, *The Child, the Family and the Outside World* (Penguin Books, first published in 1964), much of it the text of broadcast talks. It has been the best-selling of all his works, and is still the most accessible in addressing a non-psychoanalytic audience/readership.

It includes most of the chapters previously published in two separate volumes by Tavistock Publications in 1957: *The Child and the Family: First Relationships* and *The Child and the Outside World: Studies in Developing Relationships*. The second part in the second volume on children in wartime ('Children Under Stress') was omitted from *The Child, the Family and the Outside World*, but is now available with two other missing chapters, in the volume *Deprivation and Delinquency*, with another chapter, also not reprinted in the 1964 volume, on 'Aggression'. It is replaced in 1964 by a chapter titled 'Roots of Aggression', while the two chapters are side by side in *Deprivation and Delinquency*. Two further omitted chapters from *The Child and the Outside World* appear in *Society and the Growing Child*. Only 'Two Adopted Children' and 'The Impulse to Steal' from the original 1957 set have not appeared elsewhere.

The following were published or prepared for publication during his lifetime:

Winnicott, D. W. (1931) *Clinical Notes on Disorders of Childhood*. London: Heinemann.

Winnicott, D. W. (1958; second edn 1975) *Collected Papers: Through Paediatrics to Psycho-Analysis*. London: Hogarth Press.

Winnicott, D. W. (1965a) *The Family and Individual Development*. London: Tavistock Publications.

Winnicott, D. W. (1965b) *The Maturational Processes and the Facilitating Environment: Studies in the Theory of Emotional Development*. London: Hogarth Press.

Winnicott, D. W. (1971a) *Playing and Reality*. London: Routledge.

Winnicott, D. W. (1971b) *Therapeutic Consultations in Child Psychiatry*. New York: Basic Books.

Of these, *Playing and Reality* is the most immediately relevant to the general reader, and the most reasonably priced. It contains the 'Transitional Objects' and 'Adolescence' papers, making it especially useful. *Therapeutic Consultations* is only available at present in hardback, unfortunately since it contains many fascinating case histories, most of which include use of the squiggle game. It provides the best insights into Winnicott's work with children of different ages. Like *Playing and Reality* and *The Family and Individual Development*, both soft-cover books, *Through Paediatrics to Psycho-Analysis* and *The Maturational Processes and the Facilitating Environment*, consist of papers read and published at different times, many of which are referred to in my own text. *Clinical Notes on Disorders of Childhood* is a book mainly on paediatrics. Two of its most relevant papers appear in *Through Paediatrics to Psycho-Analysis*.

The remaining books under Winnicott's name are drawn from his papers, and edited variously by Clare Winnicott, Madeleine Davis and Ray Shepherd, and Christopher Bollas, Ishak Ramzy and Masud Khan:

Winnicott, D. W. (1980) *The Piggle: an Account of the Psychoanalytic Treatment of a Little Girl*. London: Penguin Books.

Winnicott, D. W. (1984) *Deprivation and Delinquency*. London: Tavistock/ Routledge.

Winnicott, D. W. (1986) *Home is Where We Start From: Essays by a Psychoanalyst*. London: Penguin Books.

Winnicott, D. W. (1988a) *Babies and Their Mothers*. London: Free Association Books.

Winnicott, D. W. (1988b) *Human Nature*. London: Free Association Books.

Winnicott, D. W. (1989a) *Holding and Interpretation: Fragment of an Analysis*. London: Karnac Books.

Winnicott, D. W. (1989b) *Psycho-Analytic Explorations*. London: Karnac Books.

My own evaluation leads me to prefer the first set of books listed, published in Winnicott's lifetime, to these later texts. *The Piggle* provides a less expensive way of viewing Winnicott's child work than *Therapeutic Consultations*. *Human Nature*, a little scrappy though it is, can be said to summarize usefully many of Winnicott's central ideas. *Home is Where We Start From* and *Babies and their Mothers* are reasonably priced, although not the most important collections of various papers. *Holding and Interpretation*, although the only long example of his own record of adult work, is by and large somewhat laboured reading. These later books are of course of interest to the serious student of Winnicott, and they are more suited to specialists and those who wish to follow his application of his psychoanalytic ideas to specific care settings and various professional groupings. We have to remember that although Winnicott was not slow to publish his papers generally, the books edited after his death consist in the main of papers to which he did not give priority (although there are one or two reprints of papers found in the books previously published). I acknowledge as I mentioned in Chapter 1, Madeleine Davis's comment on Winnicott's plan to publish 'a mixture of unpublished papers and papers from journals and anthologies' (Davis and Wallbridge, 1981: 173). But his judgement to hold them back even for the time being might have been correct, since these later works are not the essential Winnicott.

References

Anzieu, D. (ed.) (1990) *Psychic Envelopes*. London: Karnac.

Bick, E. (1968) 'The Experience of Skin in Early Object Relations', *International Journal of Psycho-Analysis*, 49, 484.

Bion, W. R. (1977) *The Seven Servants*. New York: Jason Aronson.

Bollas, C. (1987) *Shadow of the Object: Psychoanalysis of the Unthought Known*. London: Free Association Books.

Bollas, C. (1992) *Being a Character: Psychoanalysis and Self Experience*. London: Routledge.

Bollas, C. (1995) *Cracking Up: Unconscious Work in Self Experience*. London: Routledge.

Bowlby, J. (1988) *A Secure Base: Clinical Applications of Attachment Theory*. London: Routledge.

Brody, S. (1980) 'Transitional Objects: Idealization of a Phenomenon', *Psychoanalytic Quarterly*, 49, 561–605.

Bronstein, A. A. (1992) 'The Fetish, Transitional Objects, and Illusion', *Psychoanalytic Review*, 79, 2, 239–60.

Chodorow, N. (1978) *The Reproduction of Mothering and the Sociology of Gender*. Berkeley, CA: University of California Press.

Chodorow, N. (1989) *Feminism and Psychoanalytic Theory*. New Haven and London: Yale University Press.

Clancier, A. and Kalmanovitch, J. (1987) *Winnicott and Paradox: from Birth to Creation*. London: Tavistock Publications.

Clarke, A. M. and Clarke, A. D. B. (1986) 'Thirty Years of Child Psychology: a Selective Review', *Journal of Child Psychology and Psychiatry*, 27, 6, 719–59.

Cooper, J. (1993) *Speak of Me as I Am: the Life and Work of Masud Khan*. London: Karnac Books.

Davis, J. (1993) 'Winnicott as Physician', *Winnicott Studies: The Journal of the Squiggle Foundation*. 7, 95–7.

Davis, M. (1993) 'Winnicott and the Spatula Game', *Winnicott Studies: The Journal of the Squiggle Foundation*. 7, 57–67.

Davis, M. and Wallbridge, D. (1981) *Boundary and Space: an Introduction to the Work of D. W. Winnicott*. London: Karnac Books.

Dinnerstein, D. (1987) *The Rocking of the Cradle and the Ruling of the World*. London: The Women's Press.

Dockar-Drysdale, B. (1968) *Therapy in Child Care*. London: Longmans.

Dockar-Drysdale, B. (1990) *Provision of the Primary Experience: Winnicottian Work with Children and Adolescents*. London: Free Association Books.

Eigen, M. (1981) 'The Area of Faith in Winnicott, Lacan and Bion', *International Journal of Psycho-Analysis*, 62, 413–33.

150   D. W. Winnicott

Erikson, E. (1958) Young Man Luther. London: Faber.
Erikson, E. (1965) Childhood and Society. London: Penguin Books.
Farhi, N. (1992) 'D. W. Winnicott and a Personal Tradition', in L. Spurling (ed.), From the Words of My Mouth: Tradition in Psychotherapy. London: Routledge, 78–105.
Ferguson, H., Gilligan R. and Torode, R. (eds) (1993) Surviving Childhood Adversity – Issues for Policy and Practice. Trinity College, Dublin: Social Studies Press.
Ferguson, S. (1973) A Guard Within. London: Penguin Books.
Flarsheim, A. (1978) 'Discussion of Antony Flew', in S. Grolnick, L. Barkin, and W. Muensterberger (eds), Between Reality and Fantasy: Transitional Objects and Phenomena. London and New York: Jason Aronson, 505–10.
Flew, A. (1978) 'Transitional Objects and Transitional Phenomena: Comments and Interpretations', in S. Grolnick, L. Barkin, and W. Muensterberger (eds), Between Reality and Fantasy: Transitional Objects and Phenomena. London and New York: Jason Aronson, 483–501.
Freud, S. (1914) Remembering, Repeating and Working Through (Further Recommendations on the Technique of Psycho-Analysis II) (Standard edition, volume 12.) London: Hogarth Press, 147–56.
Freud, S. (1927) The Future of an Illusion. (Penguin Freud Library: Volume 12.) London: Penguin Books, 183–241.
Freud, S. (1933) New Introductory Lectures on Psychoanalysis. (Penguin Freud Library: Volume 2.) London: Penguin Books.
Freud, S. and Breuer, J. (1895) Studies on Hysteria. (Penguin Freud Library: Volume 3.) London: Penguin Books.
Fuller, P. (1988) Art and Psychoanalysis. London: Hogarth Press.
Gaddini, R. and Gaddini, E. (1970) 'Transitional Objects and the Process of Individuation: a Study in Three Different Social Groups', Journal of the American Academy of Child Psychiatry, 9, 347–65.
Greenberg, J. R. and Mitchell, S. A. (1983) Object Relations in Psychoanalytic Theory. London: Harvard University Press.
Grolnick, S. (1990) The Work and Play of Winnicott. New York: Jason Aronson.
Grolnick, S., Barkin, L. and Muensterberger, W. (eds) (1978) Between Reality and Fantasy: Transitional Objects and Phenomena. London and New York: Jason Aronson.
Grotstein, J. S. (ed.) (1981) Do I Dare Disturb the Universe? A Memorial to Wilfred R. Bion. Beverly Hills: Caesura Press.
Grotstein, J. S. (1994) 'The Poetics of Intimacy', Winnicott Studies: the Journal of the Squiggle Foundation, 9, 48–57.
Guntrip, H. (1975) 'My Experience of Analysis with Fairbairn and Winnicott', International Review of Psycho-Analysis, 2, 145–56.
Hendry, E. (1987) 'A Case Study of Play-based Work With Very Young Children', Journal of Social Work Practice, 3, 2, 1–8.
Hersov, L. (1986) 'Child Psychiatry in Britain – the Last 30 Years', Journal of Child Psychology and Psychiatry, 27, 6, 781–801.
Hobson, R. F. (1985) Forms of Feeling: the Heart of Psychotherapy. London: Tavistock.
Hopkins, J. (1990) 'The Observed Infant of Attachment Theory', British Journal of Psychotherapy, 6, 4.
Hughes, J. M. (1989) Reshaping the Psychoanalytic Domain: the Work of Melanie

Klein, W. R. D. Fairbairn and D. W. Winnicott. Los Angeles: University of California Press.

Issroff, J. (1993) 'Kitchen Therapy', *Winnicott Studies: The Journal of the Squiggle Foundation.* 7, 42–51.

Khan, M. (1974) *The Privacy of the Self: Papers on Psychoanalytic Theory and Technique.* London: Hogarth Press.

Khan, M. (1983) *Hidden Selves: Between Theory and Practice in Psychoanalysis.* London: Hogarth Press.

King, L. (1994) 'There Is No Such Thing as a Mother', *Winnicott Studies: the Journal of the Squiggle Foundation*, 9, 18–23.

King, P. and Steiner, R. (eds) (1991) *The Freud–Klein Controversies 1941–45.* London: Routledge.

Klein, M. (1975) *Envy and Gratitude and Other Works: 1946–63.* London: Hogarth Press.

Lacan, J. (1949) 'Le Stade du Miroir comme formateur de la fonction du je, telle qu'elle nous est révélée dans l'expérience psychanalytique', in *Écrits* (1966). Paris: Éditions du Seuil.

Lieberman, A. F., Weston, D. R. and Pawl, J. R. (1991) 'Preventive Intervention and Outcome with Anxiously Attached Dyads', *Child Development*, 62, 199–209.

Little, M. I. (1981) *Transference Neurosis and Transference Psychosis.* New York: Jason Aronson.

Little, M. I. (1985) 'Winnicott Working in Areas Where Psychotic Anxieties Predominate: a Personal Record', *Free Associations*, 3, 9–42.

Little, M. I. (1990) *Psychotic Anxieties and Containment: a Personal Record of an Analysis with Winnicott.* New York: Jason Aronson.

Lomas, P. (1973) *True and False Experience.* London: Allen Lane.

Lomas, P. (1987a) *The Limits of Interpretation.* London: Penguin Books.

Lomas, P. (1987b) 'Arrogant Insights' – a Review of 'The Spontaneous Gesture'. *Times Literary Supplement*, 24 July, p. 798.

Mahler, M. S., Pine, F. and Bergman, A. (1975) *The Psychological Birth of the Human Infant.* New York: Basic Books.

Mancia, M. (1993) 'The Absent Father: His Role in Sexual Deviations and in Transference', *International Journal of Psycho-Analysis*, 74, 941–50.

Meisel, P. and Kendrick, W. (1985) *Bloomsbury/Freud: the Letters of James and Alix Strachey, 1924–1925.* New York: Basic Books.

Milner, M. (1957) *On Not Being Able to Paint* (2nd edition). London: Heinemann.

Milner, M. (1969) *In the Hands of the Living God: an Account of a Psycho-Analytic Treatment.* London: Hogarth Press.

Murray, L. (1989) 'Winnicott and the Developmental Psychology of Infancy', *British Journal of Psychotherapy*, 5, 3, 333–48.

Murray, L. (1992) 'The Impact of Postnatal Depression on Infant Development', *Journal of Child Psychology and Psychiatry*, 33, 3, 543–61.

Murray, L. and Cooper, P. (1993) 'Clinical Applications of Attachment Theory and Research: Change in Infant Attachment with Brief Psychotherapy', in J. Richter (ed.), *The Clinical Application of Ethology and Attachment Theory.* Occasional Papers No. 9. London: Association for Child Psychology and Psychiatry, 15–24.

Murray, L., Fiori-Cowley, A., Hooper, R. and Cooper, P. J. (1994a) 'The Impact of Postnatal Depression and Associated Adversity on Early Mother–Infant Interactions and Later Infant Outcome' (submitted for publication).

Murray, L., Stanley, C., Hooper, R., King, F., and Fiori-Cowley, A. (1994b) 'The

Role of Infant Factors in Postnatal Depression and Mother–Infant Interactions' (submitted for publication)..

Nezworski, T., Tolan, W. J. and Belsky, J. (1988) 'Intervention in Insecure Attachment', in J. Belsky and T. Nezworski (eds), *Clinical Implications of Attachment.* Hillside, NJ: Lawrence Erlbaum.

Parker, R. (1994) 'Maternal Ambivalence', *Winnicott Studies: the Journal of the Squiggle Foundation,* 9, 3–17.

Paskauskas, R. A. (ed.) (1993) *The Complete Correspondence of Sigmund Freud and Ernest Jones 1908–1939.* Cambridge, MA.: Belknap Press.

Phillips, A. (1988) *Winnicott.* London: Fontana.

Phillips, A. (1993) *On Kissing, Tickling and Being Bored.* London: Faber.

Phillips, A. (1994) *On Flirtation.* London: Faber.

Pietroni, M. and Poupard, S. (1991) 'Direct work with Children, Their Families and Other Caretakers – the Primary Focus', in M. Pietroni (ed.), *Right or Privilege: Post Qualifying Training with Special Reference to Child Care.* London: CCETSW, 71–84.

Rayner, E. (1990) *The Independent Mind in British Psychoanalysis.* London: Free Association Books.

Riley, C. (1993) Review of Frances Tustin's 'Autistic States in Children', *Winnicott Studies: the Journal of the Squiggle Foundation,* 8, 76–83.

Rodman, F. R. (1987) *The Spontaneous Gesture: Selected Letters of D. W. Winnicott.* London: Harvard University Press.

Roudinesco, E. (1990) *Jacques Lacan and Co.: a History of Psychoanalysis in France, 1925–1985.* London: Free Association Books.

Rudnytsky, P. L. (1989) 'Winnicott and Freud', *Psychoanalytic Study of the Child,* 44, 331–50.

Rudnytsky, P. L. (1991) *The Psychoanalytic Vocation: Rank, Winnicott and the Legacy of Freud.* London: Yale University Press.

Rycroft, C. (1968) *Imagination and Reality: Psycho-Analytical Essays 1951–61.* London: Hogarth Press.

Rycroft, C. (1985) *Psychoanalysis and Beyond.* London: Chatto and Windus.

Samuels, A. (1993) *The Political Psyche.* London: Routledge.

Searles, H. (1960) *The Nonhuman Environment.* New York: International University Press.

Searles, H. (1965) *Collected Papers on Schizophrenia and Related Subjects.* London: Hogarth Press.

Seeley, S., Cooper, P. J. and Murray, L. (1995) 'Health Visitor Intervention in Postnatal Depression, an Evaluation of the Outcome for Mothers and Babies', *Health Visitors Association* (in press).

Segal, J. (1992) *Key Figures in Counselling and Psychotherapy: Melanie Klein.* London: Sage Publications.

Spensley, S. (1994) *Frances Tustin.* London: Routledge.

Spitz, R. S. (1965) *The First Year of Life.* New York: International Universities Press.

Stern, D. N. (1985) *The Interpersonal World of the Infant: a View from Psychoanalysis and Developmental Psychology.* New York: Basic Books.

Tizard, J. P. M. (1971) 'Obituary: Donald Winnicott', *International Journal of Psycho-Analysis,* 52, 3.

Treurniet, N. (1993) 'What Is Psychoanalysis Now?', *International Journal of Psycho-Analysis,* 74, 873–91.

Tustin, F. (1986) *Autistic Barriers in Neurotic Patients.* London: Karnac Books.

Tustin, F. (1990) *The Protective Shell in Children and Adults*. London: Karnac Books.

Tustin, F. (1992) *Autistic States in Children* (revised edition). London: Routledge.

Usuelli, A. K. (1992) 'The Significance of Illusion in the Work of Freud and Winnicott: a Controversial Issue', *International Review of Psycho-Analysis*, 19, 179–87.

Varma, V. P. (1992) *The Secret Life of Vulnerable Children*. London: Routledge.

Winnicott, C. (1964) *Child Care and Social Work*. Welwyn, Herts: Codicote Press.

Winnicott, C. (1968) 'Communicating with Children', in R. J. N. Tod (ed.), *Disturbed Children*. London: Longmans, 65–80.

Winnicott, D. W. (1931) *Clinical Notes on Disorders of Childhood*. London: Heinemann.

Winnicott, D. W. (1957) *The Child and the Outside World: Studies in Developing Relationships*. London: Tavistock Publications.

Winnicott, D. W. (1960) 'String', *Journal of Child Psychology and Psychiatry*, 1, 49–52.

Winnicott, D. W. (1963) 'Training for Child Psychiatry', *Journal of Child Psychology and Psychiatry*, 4, 85–91.

Winnicott, D. W. (1964) *The Child, the Family and the Outside World*. London: Penguin Books.

Winnicott, D. W. (1965a) *The Family and Individual Development*. London: Tavistock Publications.

Winnicott, D. W. (1965b) *The Maturational Processes and the Facilitating Environment: Studies in the Theory of Emotional Development*. London: Hogarth Press.

Winnicott, D. W. (1969) 'James Strachey: Obituary', *International Journal of Psycho-Analysis*, 50, 129–31.

Winnicott, D. W. (1971a) *Playing and Reality*. London: Routledge.

Winnicott, D. W. (1971b) *Therapeutic Consultations in Child Psychiatry*. New York: Basic Books.

Winnicott, D. W. (1975) *Collected Papers: Through Paediatrics to Psycho-Analysis* (2nd edn). London: Tavistock Publications. First published 1958.

Winnicott, D. W. (1980) *The Piggle: an Account of the Psychoanalytic Treatment of a Little Girl*. London: Penguin Books.

Winnicott, D. W. (1984) *Deprivation and Delinquency*. London: Tavistock/Routledge.

Winnicott, D. W. (1986) *Home is Where We Start From: Essays by a Psychoanalyst*. London: Penguin Books.

Winnicott, D. W. (1988a) *Babies and Their Mothers*. London: Free Association Books.

Winnicott, D. W. (1988b) *Human Nature*. London: Free Association Books.

Winnicott, D. W. (1989a) *Holding and Interpretation: Fragment of an Analysis*. London: Karnac Books.

Winnicott, D. W. (1989b) *Psycho-Analytic Explorations*. London: Karnac Books.

Index